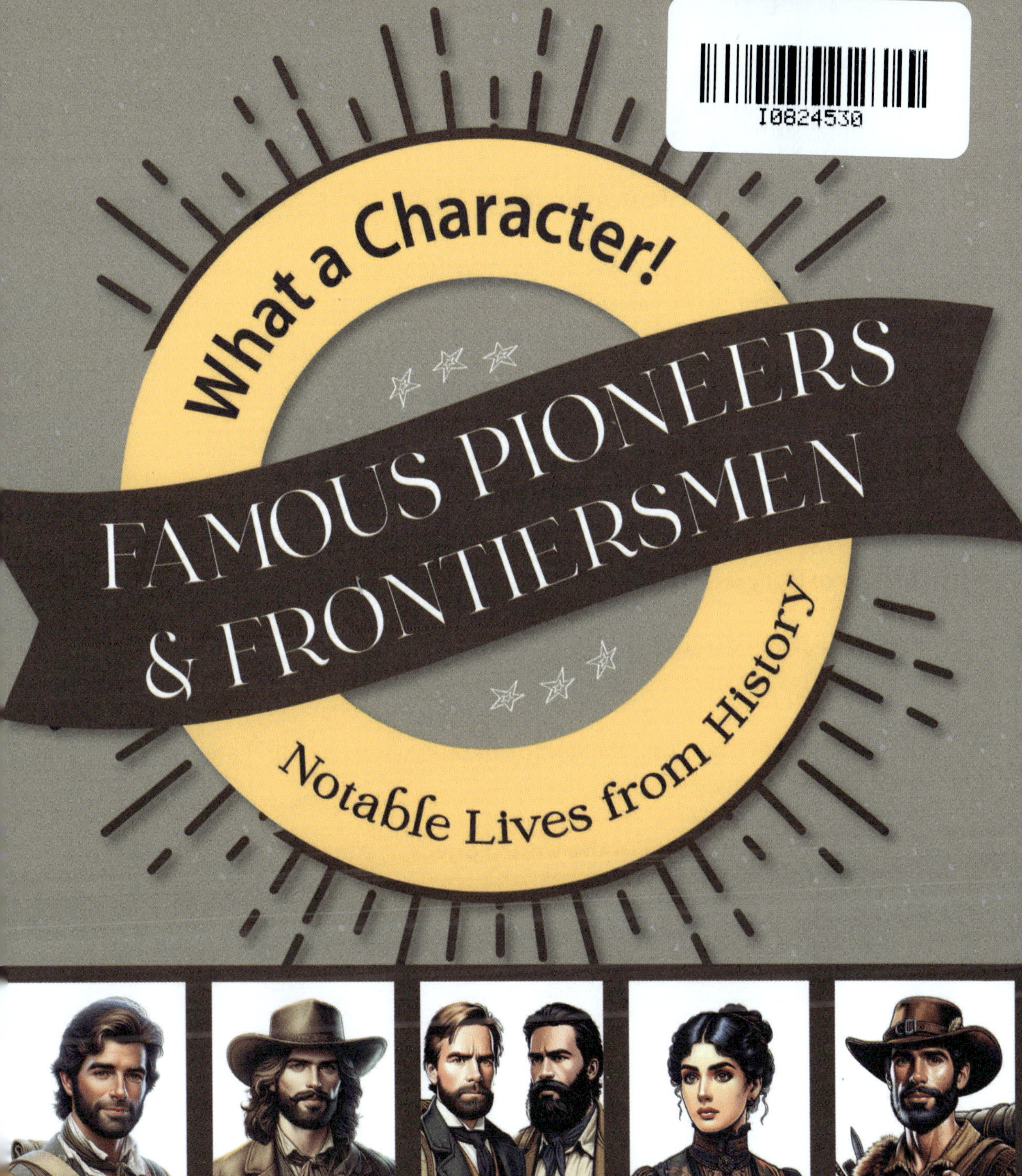

Marilyn Boyer

First printing: July 2024
Second printing: April 2025

Master Books, P.O. Box 726, Green Forest, AR 72638

Master Books® is a division of the New Leaf Publishing Group, LLC.

ISBN: 978-1-68344-366-7
ISBN: 978-1-61458-881-8 (digital)
Library of Congress Control Number: 2024938827

Cover: Diana Bogardus
Interior: Terry White

Please consider requesting that a copy of this volume be purchased by your local library system.

Printed in the United States of America

Please visit our website for other great titles:
www.masterbooks.com

For information regarding promotional opportunities,
please contact the publicity department at pr@nlpg.com.

Table of Contents

PUBLISHER'S NOTE: Throughout this book, we have made efforts to use culturally appropriate terminology when referring to the Native Peoples of the Americas. However, in certain instances, the term *Indian* may appear within quotations or historical references, particularly in relation to the time period discussed or events such as the "French and Indian War." Our intent with this series is to convey respect and accuracy in our portrayal of historical events and peoples. We invite readers to approach these references with an understanding of the context in which they are presented and to engage thoughtfully with the narratives shared within this book.

Image Credits

Images are AI-generated at shutterstock.com

Maps:

Map Trek: page 4 and 90.

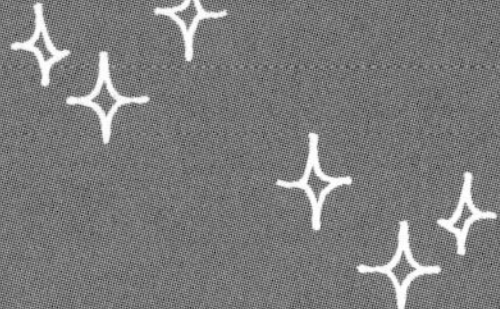

Introduction

Just 200 years ago, much of what would become the United States was still a rugged, untamed frontier. Stories were just being written of the daring pioneers, resilient frontiersmen, and legendary mountain men who carved their paths through the wilderness and shaped the course of American history. From the early days of westward expansion to the height of the fur trade era, these brave souls ventured into the unknown, facing countless challenges and forging a legacy that continues to inspire us today.

Many of the courageous men and women living at that time left behind the comforts of civilization to explore new territories, establish settlements, and trade with Native American communities. These people daily witnessed the beauty and brutality of life on the frontier, where every day brought fresh opportunities and dangers.

The conflicts of this life were often rooted in worldviews. The Native peoples lived close to nature, most often taking only what was needed, and many traveled large distances during the seasons of the year in search of food and other resources. Some had their own informal territories and agreements with other tribes, but the concept of owning the land as individuals as colonists did was not one in which they usually lived by. Clashes between pioneers and the Native peoples occurred over resources and viewpoints. Many generations of the Native peoples had lived on these lands with deep cultural connections to it. Now these new people were saying it was only for them and the Native peoples needed to stay away.

Among the heroes of the American frontier were the pioneers, who blazed trails through dense forests, crossed treacherous rivers, and braved harsh weather conditions in search of a better life and the opportunity for more land to own. Whether traveling in covered wagons along the Oregon Trail or seeking gold in the California Gold Rush, these individuals embodied the spirit of adventure and strength that defined the American West.

No story of the Wild West would be complete without the fearless frontiersmen who made their homes on the edge of civilization, defending their land against thieves and the harsh realities of nature. With their expert marksmanship and survival skills, these rugged individuals became legends of the frontier, earning respect and admiration from settlers and sometimes even Native Americans alike.

Finally, there were the mountain men, solitary wanderers who roamed the remote wilderness in search of beaver pelts and other valuable furs. Living off the land and trading with fur companies, these tough adventurers carved out a solitary existence in some of the most inhospitable regions of North America. Their tales of survival, independence, and encounters with wildlife capture the essence of life on the untamed frontier.

1

Daniel Boone – Blazing the Wilderness Trail

1734–1820	Virginia–Kentucky

Who Was Daniel Boone?

Daniel Boone was born on October 22, 1734, before there was a United States of America. At that time, there were 13 colonies that belonged to England. Daniel's family lived in the colony of Pennsylvania. They were Quakers — peace-loving people. Daniel was the sixth child to be born to Squire and Sarah Boone, who eventually would have 12 children. Daniel grew up loving to be outdoors, especially in the woods.

Daniel was a hard worker. In 1744, when his father bought a big pasture for grazing his herd, Daniel took the responsibility of caring for the animals. He loved the job. When he wasn't guarding the herd, he was hunting. Daniel was alert to signs of wildlife. He developed a friendship with the Delaware tribe, who taught him much about the ways of the wilderness. They taught him how to track, hunt, and survive in the forest, including how to stay warm in the snow. Daniel soon began wearing **buckskin** clothes instead of Quaker garb. Daniel's father gave him his first long rifle when he turned 13. Daniel became the best shot in the whole family.

buckskin: Made from the skin of a deer

During the fall and winter, Daniel would head off by himself to hunt and trap, to supply the family with meat. Animal skins were made into blankets, clothing, and rugs as well. Daniel's skill meant that his family would never starve or freeze. Daniel was always generous to those who needed meat or skins, and people began to respect him. His father taught him carpentry skills. He learned to repair wagons and tools and even build a house.

When Daniel was 14, his sister-in-law taught him how to read and write. Daniel became a devoted reader. He often read books at night while he sat around the campfire. Where he really excelled was in the woods. He hardly ever got lost, knew animal tracks, and listened carefully for sounds around him. He killed his first bear when he was 15 years old.

Time to Move West

Squire Boone felt that the land was getting too crowded with settlers. He decided to move his family south, where the farmland was inexpensive and fertile. The Boones placed all their belongings in a covered wagon and headed for Virginia in 1750. There were no

roads, only rough trails. Daniel, the best woodsman, led his family to Winchester, Virginia, 500 miles away. The family lived there for about a year before heading for the unsettled Yadkin Valley in North Carolina.

Daniel left on what was called a "long hunt," a Native term meaning a hunting trip that lasted for the entire fall and part of winter. For the rest of his life, he would go on "long hunts" every year. One autumn, Daniel killed many bears. In this way he helped to feed and clothe his family; he made money selling his beaver and otter skins as well. For his entire life, hunting was Daniel's main source of income.

War Times

While attending a friend's wedding when he was 19 years old, Daniel met 15-year-old Rebecca Bryan. Rebecca reminded Daniel of his mother, and the couple began spending a lot of time together. Daniel wanted to get married, but the French and Indian War was gearing up. Daniel was 20 years old when he joined the British army to protect his family's land. Before he left, his father said, "I've never been to war myself, son, but I know if you do the kind of job you're capable of doing, then you'll come out just fine. And we're all proud of you."[1]

blacksmith: Person who makes and repairs things made of iron

Daniel served as a **blacksmith** and supply wagon driver under British General Edward Braddock. Braddock knew nothing of frontier life or how the Native People fought. He had his men dress in bright blue or red uniforms and stand in long, straight lines to fire at the enemy. The American soldiers tried to tell him how to fight the Native American way, but he would not listen.

Daniel appealed to one of the officers, "Sir, I think we should not stay too long in this place. We're in the lowlands and the fort's at the top. It makes us good targets."[2] In a few moments, they were under attack. Braddock ended up dying; three hours later, 977 British soldiers lay dead or wounded. The wagons were robbed, and prisoners were taken to the fort and killed. Daniel, as a wagon driver, had not taken part in the battle but watched horror-stricken as men fell before his eyes. Someone who knew him later wrote, "He had very little of the war spirit."[3]

Kanta-ke

One friend Daniel met in the army was John Findley, a hunter. John told him of the wonderful lands beyond the Appalachian Mountains. The Iroquois called the land 'Kanta-ke,' what we know today as Kentucky. Wild elk, buffalo, bear, turkey, and deer roamed freely there, and geese were abundant. People had not settled there yet. It sounded like paradise to Daniel, but it would have to wait for a while.

When he left the army, he went home and married Rebecca. He was 21 now and she was 17. They had a big wedding and Daniel built them a log house on their own little farm. A year later baby James was born. Nine more children would be born to the couple. Daniel once said, "There are three things a man needs to be happy. A good gun, a good horse, and a good family."[4] The life Rebecca faced was not an easy one. If there had not been women who were brave and determined like their husbands, the West would have remained unsettled.

Daniel loved his family, but he did miss the woods. One day John Findley showed up again at Daniel's door. He spent the winter with the Boone family. He was excited to fill Daniel in on the Kentucky land. On May 1, 1769, Daniel, his brother Squire, his brother-in-law John Stuart, John Findley, and three of Daniel's neighbors set off for the "promised land." Equipped with their long rifles, salt, kettles, traps, food, blankets, and bear skins, they headed off through the forest. The trip took about five weeks. Upon arriving, they established a base on Station Camp Creek in Kentucky. Daniel later said this was the

happiest time of his life. At night Daniel would sit by the campfire and read his Bible. Hunting provided abundant supplies of pelts and skins from which he hoped to make enough profit to pay for this trip.

Troubles

A band of Shawnee people came into camp and eyed the huge pile of animal skins Daniel and his partners had been collecting all winter. The Shawnee took the skins, the horses, and the men's rifles. Daniel and John were held prisoner for seven days. When the Shawnee released them, they gave them small guns, **moccasins**, one deerskin, and a small supply of gunpowder to allow them to hunt for food. The chief let them go, telling them to leave the land and go home. Daniel later reported that the chief had acted "in the most friendly manner."[5]

The two men did not go home but stayed for the next winter to try to make up for their losses. They lived in a cave and hunted and trapped, but one day John went out to hunt and never returned. Daniel **surmised** that he had been killed by Native People. Daniel now had no companions but his

moccasins: Soft leather shoes made by Native Americans

surmised: Guessed

three dogs to whom he sang and talked. After almost two years, Daniel had about $700 worth of furs and decided it was time to return home. When he was only two days away from home, a group of Cherokees seized his pile of furs. He was disappointed about all that income lost, but at least he had his life. He was ready to get home now.

Home Again

When Daniel got home, Rebecca and the family were at a dance in town. Daniel walked quietly up behind Rebecca and asked if he might have a dance. Looking at the scruffy, dirty man before her, she declined. Daniel told her she had danced with him many times, and then she recognized her husband, screamed, and threw herself into his arms. She thought he was probably dead by now. People gathered around Daniel and wanted to hear all about the land out west. Rebecca made Daniel promise to stay home for a long time.

Moving Again

After a few years, Daniel was unhappy with how built-up things were getting. He mentioned to Rebecca the possibility of gathering a group of settlers and traveling together to the **bountiful** land of Kentucky. On September 25, 1773, a group of 50 settlers — men, women, and children — packed their wagons and began their journey beyond the hills.

The going was very slow. They were getting close to the Cumberland Gap, which was a passage through the Cumberland Mountains between Kentucky, Tennessee, and Virginia. Daniel realized at the **pace** they were going, they would likely run out of food before reaching their destination. He sent his 16-year-old son James and some others to head back for more supplies. Unfortunately, the men were attacked by some of the Native Peoples, and James was killed. Only two of the men escaped. Daniel and Rebecca were **devastated**. The rest of the party lost heart and headed back to the Yadkin Valley in North Carolina. This left the Boones alone, without a house. They spent the winter with friends in western Virginia.

bountiful: Plentiful

pace: Speed

devastated: Heartbroken and discouraged

Try Again

In March of 1775, Daniel led a group of 30 men to build bridges and level the trail called **The Wilderness Road**. Daniel's men trusted him completely. As one said, "He was our pilot and conductor through the wilderness."[6] Each morning, Daniel would mark the trail for the men to clear and then head off to hunt for game to feed them that night. By April, the group had reached the middle of Kentucky. The Wilderness Road had opened the pathway for settlers to follow safely. Over the next few years, more than 300,000 people traveled on the road.

The Wilderness Road: The path through Cumberland Gap that Daniel Boone had created

Upon their arrival, the first order of business was to build a fort. Daniel chose a spot near the Kentucky River. This location was chosen because it would control the gateway to the west. It took three years to complete the fort. The settlers stayed in the fort for the first year, but then began to claim land and spread out. They named their settlement Boonesborough, after Daniel Boone, their leader. Daniel

returned in June to bring his family to the new settlement. He had built them a new cabin with a wooden floor and windows made from real glass.

Attack

One summer day in 1776, the Shawnees and Cherokees combined forces and snuck up on the settlement. They captured three girls who had been canoeing. One was Daniel's 13-year-old daughter Jemima. Daniel and the men moved swiftly to try to rescue the girls before the warriors made it back to their camp, where Daniel and his men would be vastly outnumbered. Jemima had learned many useful things from her father. She came up with a plan. She told the girls to break branches along the way and to tear off threads from their skirts to mark their path. Daniel recognized the signs the girls had left. After three days, they saw the Native camp just ahead. Daniel and the men were able to rescue the girls. Daniel said to his men, "Thank Almighty **Providence**, boys, for we have the girls safe."[7]

Providence: God's guidance

The Fort Is Saved

About a year later, Daniel and some of the men went to a place where there were **salt springs**. Wild animals would gather there to lick salt. The men planned to camp there for several weeks. They would heat water in large kettles until it boiled away, leaving only salt. They planned to take the salt back to Boonesborough. But Daniel and his men were captured by the Shawnees.

salt springs: Saltwater springs

Daniel told the men to follow the Native People, and they would try to escape later to warn the people at Boonesborough. Chief Blackfish, the Shawnees' leader, liked and respected Daniel. He wanted to adopt him as a son. He gave him the name of Big Turtle. Daniel and his men stayed with the Shawnees that winter. They knew when spring came the Native warriors were planning to attack the fort at Boonesborough. Someone had to escape in time to warn their families.

Daniel was praying for the right opportunity. It came when the Native warriors needed salt and had taken Daniel to the salt springs with them. Suddenly, a gigantic flock of turkeys flew overhead. For a moment, the warriors forgot all about keeping their eye on Daniel. He made a mad dash for the woods and kept on running for four days. He covered 160 miles and had only one meal during the time. Exhausted and half-starved, he finally reached the fort.

He found the fort badly prepared to defend itself and at once set about preparations to make it secure. The men were ready to fight. The siege of Boonesborough lasted for 10 long, terrible days. The men in the fort had no sleep but somehow managed to beat back the attackers. Amazingly, on the 11th day, the settlers found that the Native People, having lost so many of their own, had left and gone home!

On to Missouri

One day, Daniel found out he had been too busy to file the paperwork on his land. The government said it did not belong to him. He was heartbroken, considering all he had gone through to open the Wilderness Road for others. He heard of land out west, present-day Missouri. Daniel, Rebecca, three sons and their wives, two daughters and their husbands, 17 grandchildren, and some other relatives made the long trip. He and his family built a new home there. Daniel hunted

and sold many furs and skins to provide for his family, as he always had done.

In 1800, the United States Congress voted to grant Daniel Boone a tract of 1,000 acres to reward him for all his work exploring and settling the West. He hunted, fished, and trapped for the rest of his life, and enjoyed his family. Daniel Boone will always be remembered as the man who **paved** the way to Kentucky.

Toward the end of his life, when he was 85 years old, Daniel wrote to his sister, assuring her that he was ready when the time came to meet his Maker: "All the religion I have is to love and fear God, believe in Jesus Christ, do all the good to my neighbor and myself that I can, and do as little harm as I can help, and trust on God's mercy for the rest."[8]

paved: Opened up

George Rogers Clark – The Hero of Vincennes

1778–1779	Vincennes, Indiana

Who Was George Rogers Clark?

George Rogers Clark was born on November 19, 1752, in Albemarle County, Virginia, near Charlottesville. When George was five years old, his family moved to a farm in Caroline County, Virginia. For years, the British fought the French for land in the West. Britain had won the French and Indian War, and now settlers were moving west every day. Trappers told stories of plentiful hunting, and beautiful streams and rivers. When George was 19 years old, he decided he would leave home. His father asked him how he planned to make a living. George answered, "By **surveying**. You taught me how and I have Grandfather's instruments. There will be plenty of land to measure for other people. Perhaps I'll find some to mark for my own."[9]

surveying: Establishing boundaries for a plot of land

On His Own

By June 1772, George was at Fort Pitt in Pittsburgh floating down the Ohio River. The land was sparsely settled there. George loved the land and soon found some to claim as his own. It lay along Fish Creek, a stream that flowed into the Ohio River. Here, he

spent the fall hunting, fishing, and clearing the land. When spring came, he planted corn. While it was growing, he explored 170 miles down the Ohio River and was back when his corn was waist high. He spent the next winter hunting, trapping, selling his furs, and surveying for friends and neighbors. People up and down the river were getting to know him. Clark was asked to survey lands in Kentucky. He had heard so much about the fine land that he was glad to head west.

Kentucky

James Harrod welcomed him to Harrodsburg, Kentucky, a group of cabins surrounded by a **stockade**. George was impressed with the land. James told him the only problem was trouble with the Native American tribes who rightfully considered Kentucky their hunting grounds, but the wave of settlers did not stop. Clark made Harrodsburg his headquarters and from there, took on many surveying jobs.

stockade: A fortification around a town

While he was in Harrodsburg, the American War of Independence began. The colonists wanted freedom from England's **oppressive** laws. Clark knew there could be trouble with the Native Americans whom the British **coaxed** to fight on their side. The people of Harrodsburg met and voted to send George Rogers Clark to Williamsburg, Virginia, to request ammunition and supplies.

A New Governor

When Clark reached Williamsburg, he found out that Patrick Henry, a **staunch** Patriot, had replaced British governor Lord Dunmore. Clark met with Governor Henry to make his request. He promised that the people of Kentucky would help protect Virginia in return. Henry and his council voted to send 500 pounds of gunpowder to Fort Pitt. From there it would have to make the rest of the trip by boat.

oppressive: Unjustly hard

coaxed: Persuaded

staunch: Committed

When Clark arrived at Fort Pitt, he found his cousin Joseph Rogers waiting for him with some money his father had sent. Clark used the money to hire a boat and crew. As they proceeded down the Ohio River, they were spotted by Native Americans who began chasing them. They paddled furiously and reached a spot where they could quickly roll the **kegs** of gunpowder up a hill to hide them safely in a cave. The Native Americans took their boat, but the gunpowder was safe.

Making Their Own Laws

Clark sent messages not only to Harrodsburg but to other surrounding settlements in Kentucky, telling them Virginia had agreed to let the settlers in Kentucky be a county of Virginia. They would be able to make some of their own laws. Kentuckians formed a **militia** and elected George Rogers Clark as their major. He was only 24 years old at the time. It was the job of the militia to protect all the settlements in the wilderness.

kegs: Barrels

militia: Civilian military force

fraught: Filled

1777 was **fraught** with attacks from Native Americans. The British were supplying them with guns and ammunition, encouraging them to attack. Clark realized the militia was not large enough to defend the whole territory. He came up with a plan and set off again to see Governor Patrick Henry of Virginia. Clark's plan was to lead an expedition to attack British frontier outposts in the Illinois country. The plan would depend on support from Virginia to supply ammunition and men. Henry approved the plan. He said, "Go, my dear sir, raise your companies, and I will make you a Colonel. You will do this for the defense of Virginia and Kentucky."[10]

The Long Knives

Over the next few months, Clark recruited 150 frontiersmen. The Native Americans gave them the name "The Long Knives," because their hunting knives were extremely long. Only a few officers knew what their mission was. Governor Henry had not revealed the details to the Virginia General Assembly that they would attack British outposts. He told Clark, "You are to take especial care to keep the true destination of your force secret. Its success depends upon this."[11]

Clark's men wore fur caps and shirts made from deerskin. They started down the Ohio River toward the Falls of the Ohio and set up camp at Corn Island. Here Clark told all the men the nature of their mission — that they would attack. Their first stop would be the British fort at Kaskaskia. It was July 4, 1778. There was a dance going on at the fort.

Clark stepped quietly into the room, leaned against the door, and watched the dance. A Native American man saw him and raised an alarm. Everyone looked at the stranger, frightened. Clark calmly said, "Do not be alarmed. I shall not hurt you. Go on with your dance. But remember, you are dancing under the flag of Virginia, and not under the flag of England."[12] Behind him came his men who took all the soldiers' guns. Thus, they took over the fort without a single shot being fired. When Clark told the **Kaskaskians** that France had just agreed to send money and men to help the Patriots, they all cheered "Liberty, liberty!" They decided to become part of the United States.

Kaskaskians: Native Americans who were from the area we call Illinois

Vincennes

Fort Sackville was located at Vincennes, 200 miles away on the Wabash River. This was the fort where the British gave guns and ammunition to the Native Americans who had raided Kentucky. Clark knew he must capture this fort as well. Clark met a French priest named Father Gibault. He had preached before at Vincennes, and offered to go on ahead and talk to the people to tell them the Americans were their friends.

He advised them to take down the British flag and raise the American flag in its place — otherwise, Clark and his men would attack them. The French in Vincennes agreed to do so. Again, the fort was captured without bloodshed. The British, however, were not happy. They marched down under the command of British Colonel Hamilton and recaptured Fort Sackville. Clark was determined to retake the fort. The women of Kaskaskia tribe, wanting to help, sewed flags to give to Clark. They gathered blankets and mittens for the men. Father Gibault prayed for the army's success.

Recaptured

It was winter, however, and the Wabash River had overflowed its banks. Much of the country was underwater. Vincennes was in the center of a shallow swamp of freezing water. Hamilton thought he was safe for the winter. Clark set out with his men carrying their long rifles. They faced cold blustery days and steady downpours of rain. Every night, they built fires to warm themselves and hunted for dry spots to sleep on. A third of Clark's army was sick with chills and fever. Those who were healthy cut down trees to make a boat. When they came within four miles of the fort, the water was waist-deep and icy cold. Some would have to ride their horses through the flooded river. "Wade in and follow me!" cried Clark.[13]

Clark picked up a small drummer boy and placed him on his shoulders, telling him to beat the drum. Then Clark plunged into the icy deep. When the water was too high, the drummer boy used his drum as a raft. This cheered the frozen men. His men followed and after a few hours of hard riding, they crossed the flood and stood before the fort. Colonel Hamilton, amazed, said, "They are mad, or else they had wings to cross at such a time."[14]

Clark told his men, "Cut young trees and we will fasten our flags to them. We will march in a zigzag line behind the bushes and trees. The British will think we have many more men than we do."[15] The Americans waited until they were close to the fort before firing the cannons that they had hauled down the river by flatboat. By the end of the night, they had used up every bit of their powder. Two Frenchmen who had volunteered to help them, came to the rescue, bringing them powder that they had buried in caves months ago.

Clark sent Hamilton a message in the morning advising him to surrender. Hamilton responded, "We are not disposed to be awed into any action unworthy of British subjects."[16] The Americans resumed firing and Hamilton requested a three-day **truce**. After the three days, the fighting started again. It was not long until Hamilton finally surrendered the fort. The flag of England was again hauled down, this time for good. Clark said, "From this day on, this will be called Fort Patrick Henry."[17]

truce: A cease-fire

The roar of a 13-gun salute echoed through the fort — one for each of the 13 stars of the American flag now flying over Vincennes.

This is how all the great Northwest Territory came into the possession of the Americans. The states of Ohio, Indiana, Illinois, Michigan, Wisconsin, and part of Minnesota are a part of the United States due chiefly to the efforts of George Rogers Clark, the great frontiersman.

When George Rogers Clark was an old man, some citizens from Virginia came to see him. They presented him with a beautiful sword. The blade bore these words: "Presented by the State of Virginia to her beloved son George Rogers Clark, who by the conquest of Illinois and St. Vincennes, extended her empire and aided in the defense of her liberties."[18] A marble dome held up by 16 columns stands today on the **Wabash River**. Murals are on its walls depicting the conquest of the West. A bronze statue of George Rogers Clark stands in the center of the room, looking out over the Northwest Territory he helped to win for his country.

Wabash River: The southward flowing tributary of the Ohio River

Elizabeth Zane – Frontier Girl Who Saved Fort Henry

1782	Fort Henry, Ohio Country

Fort Henry was a small frontier settlement where Wheeling, West Virginia, now stands. The fort was attacked by the native tribe of the Delaware. The Delawares were joined by a party of 100 Shawnee warriors and 200 British Rangers. A man named Simon Girty was an early settler who had sided with the British and had joined up with a group of Native Americans who were British sympathizers. Girty's family had been captured by the Senecas, who later adopted him. Girty served as an interpreter for the British to the Native Americans and led several sieges on American forts. His name was feared by settlers as being **ruthless** in his dealings with settlers.

Who Was Elizabeth (Betty) Zane?

Elizabeth, better known as Betty Zane, was the sister of Colonel Ebenezer Zane, a hunter and explorer who had braved the wilderness to find a settlement in the Western Ohio Valley. He returned to his home in Berkley County, Virginia, and persuaded several other men, including his brothers and brother-in-law, to help him build a settlement in the fine green Ohio country. When cabins were built, the men moved their families there. The settlers built a fort to protect folks from any unfriendly Native American tribes and named it Fort Henry in honor of Patrick Henry.

ruthless: Showing no compassion

The Zane brothers were known for their skill and knowledge of Native American warfare. They were powerful, rugged men with dark eyes and long dark hair. Their father had come to America from Denmark and moved to Virginia. When they were boys, they were captured by the Wyandot people, and held as captives for two years. One of the brothers, Andrew, had been killed while attempting to escape. Ebenezer, Silas, and Jonathan Zane had been **ransomed**, after two years. The youngest brother, Isaac, however, was loved by a princess of the Huron tribe. He had tried to escape several times but was always brought back and hadn't been seen by his family for four years.

Elizabeth, or Betty Zane, the only sister, was living with an aunt in Philadelphia where she was being educated. She came to live with her brother, Ebenezer, when her aunt died and **resided** at his two-story home at the settlement. The Zane brothers were proud of their sister. Betty was mischievous and had a strong will. Colonel Zane praised his sister's skill in preparing **flax** and weaving, as well as cooking. Betty sang in their little church on Sundays. She also planned and taught classes on Sundays. Betty did everything well, he said, from playing checkers to baking pies. He had told all the people in the settlement "that she could ride like a Native (person) and shoot with undoubted skill."[19] She kept a pet bear cub who had been orphaned, along with pet squirrels and pigeons. Betty loved to ride her pony, paddle her canoe, and roam the woods.

ransomed: Released after paying money

resided: Lived

flax: Flowering plant for linen production

Trouble Brewing

Colonel Zane had a good relationship with many of the Native American tribes. Settlers often consulted him to help **avert** trouble. Ebenezer's brother-in-law had just come back from Fort Pitt with the message that trouble was brewing. There was unrest among the Wyandot and Shawnee tribes. He believed trouble wouldn't necessarily come to them because Fort Henry was so well protected, but precautions had to be taken.

Fort Henry stood on a bluff overlooking the river. It was surrounded by a **stockade fence** that was 12 feet high. The **blockhouse** was two stories high with thick oak walls. There were small openings in the walls for manning guns. There were also several cabins inside the walls. The settlers began to move possessions and supplies inside the fort to keep them protected from Native Americans. The women were busy caring for the children; they also cleaned rifles and molded bullets to aid their husbands.

avert: Avoid

stockade fence: Protective barrier

blockhouse: Observation tower

Colonel Zane hadn't moved into the fort since his house was well-built and he planned to defend it. He did move his cattle and horses inside the walls, however. A new settler, Alfred Clark, who had left Virginia after his

father died, came down from Fort Pitt in Pennsylvania to help Colonel Zane. He was strong and not afraid of work, but new to the frontier life. Colonel Zane, a good judge of character, liked the young man. He gave Alfred a rifle so he could patrol and watch for danger.

Isaac Returns and Is Captured Again

Alfred was returning from his patrol when he heard Colonel Zane's dog barking furiously. He observed a log floating down the river with a man clinging to it. The man was nearly drowned! Alfred rescued him from the river and asked him his name. The man managed to gasp, "Zane." Alfred ran to find Colonel Zane. Upon investigation, the Colonel realized the man was his son, Isaac, who had escaped from the Hurons again. The dog had recognized him, so he was barking furiously. Colonel Zane sent Alfred to get Betty. She was thrilled to find her brother was still alive. She threw her arms around her beloved Isaac. He had been her constant companion when they were young children. "I have prayed and prayed that you would be restored to us," she cried.[20]

Everyone was **spellbound** as Isaac told of all his experiences with the tribe that evening. The summer passed uneventfully. The Zanes were glad to have Isaac home again. He and Alfred became good friends and spent many hours together. However, while out in the

spellbound: Fascinated

woods one day, Isaac was again captured and returned to the Huron camp. The chief of the tribe told Isaac that he must marry his daughter and become one of the tribe or he would be killed. Isaac was torn. He wanted to be home with his family, but he knew that for now, he must remain with the Hurons.

Siege of Fort Henry

Life went on amid the many dangers of the wilderness. In the summer of 1777, rumors surfaced that Simon Girty and his band of warriors and British rangers were preparing to attack Fort Henry. Colonel Sheppard was in charge of the fort at the time. He had only 40 men to defend it. He sent out a **reconnoitering** party to find out the enemy position. The party was **ambushed**, and more than half of them were killed. Another party was sent out to help, but most of them were also killed. This put the fort in great danger. Women and children were in the fort but surrounded by the enemy. The situation seemed desperate.

reconnoitering: Group of men sent to gather information

ambushed: Attacked from a concealed position

Colonel Sheppard, though, was not one to surrender easily. He called the remaining men to him and said, "We must defend this fort to the last man. If we surrender, it means sure death to us all . . . and the women and children will suffer most. Let each man do his full duty, and women must help."[21]

Simon Girty came, demanding that the fort surrender. He threatened to kill every man, woman, and child. He gave the order for the warriors to attack. Some of the log huts belonging to the settlers but located outside the fort provided protection for the native warriors. But the settlers were all **sure shots**. Because they were low on powder, they made sure every shot counted. The Native Americans withdrew after six hours to a nearby location. For a short time, the fighting **ceased.** During this **lull**, someone brought word that the powder supply was nearly gone. There was only enough to last for one hour of battle. After that, the settlers would be at the mercy of the enemy.

The women were **casting** bullets, carefully measuring the powder from their limited

sure shots: Skilled in shooting

lull: Temporary quiet time

casting: Making in a mold

supply, and loading the rifles for the men. Sixteen-year-old Betty joined the women in this task. Face dark from charcoal dust; Betty knelt before the charcoal fire blowing it with the **bellows**. Her friend, Lydia, was kneeling by her side, holding a bullet mold on a block of wood. Betty lifted the ladle from the red coals and poured the hot metal into the mold. She worked carefully. Too much or too little lead would make an imperfect ball that would misfire. Her friend dipped the mold in a bucket of water, removed it, and beat it on the floor. Out rolled a small shiny lead bullet. Betty rubbed it with a greasy rag and popped it into a jar. For 40 hours the girls continued in this fashion without sleep or rest and very little food.

bellows: Device for blowing on a fire

Powder Supply

Ebenezer Zane's house was about 60 yards outside the fort's walls. He had a keg of powder stored there. Colonel Sheppard said someone must be sent to retrieve the powder despite the great risk, but who would go? The Native Americans just outside the fort were in easy gunshot range. It most certainly meant death for anyone who would attempt to go. He said he would not order anyone to go but would ask for volunteers. Several men at once offered their service, but just then Betty Zane stepped forward. "No man can be spared now. We have too few to defend this place. I am the one to go. Unbar the gate and let me out."[22]

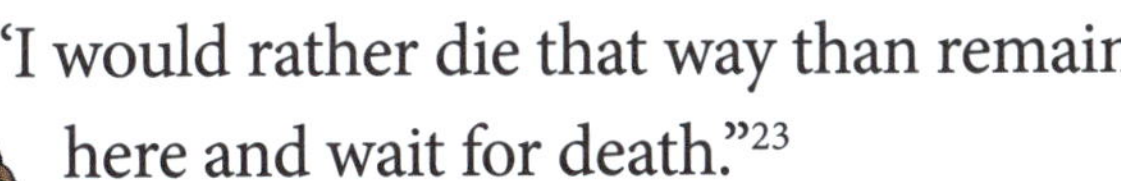

"I would rather die that way than remain here and wait for death."[23]

Colonel Sheppard hesitated. One of the settlers present said, "It ain't a bad plan. Betty can run like a deer. And bein' a woman, they may let her get to the cabin without shootin'."[24] Suddenly all weariness left Betty. Her eyes shone with **resolve** and a spirit of hopefulness. The colonel thought it was possible. Maybe she could save the fort! If she failed, she would at least be spared the terrible type of death that awaited them all.

resolve:
Determination

Betty's Heroism

The heavy gate was opened. Betty ran out, looking straight ahead. The warriors looked on in wonder, supposing she was coming to them as a captive. Betty sprang into the house and grabbed the keg. Colonel Zane said, "Brave girl, so help me God, you are going to do it. I know you can run. Run as you never ran in all your life."[25] Betty reappeared at the door. She ran with all her might. Shrieking and yelling fiercely, the warriors began to run after her, firing at her as they ran. Bullets flew all around Betty, striking the ground near her feet and buzzing over her head. None but a fine marksman had a chance to hit that small figure as she sped like lightning toward the gate.

Betty saw the gate swing open and the figure of her brother cheering her on. Only a few more yards to go! Stumbling, she was caught up in the arms of her friends as she heard the gate slam shut. "We have a heroine in this fort, and now we conquer or die!" cried the men as they ran to their posts with the newly supplied powder.

Siege Ends

The Native Americans, realizing they had lost a golden opportunity, rushed on the fort only to be met with unceasing cannon fire. They fell back. The settlers, with renewed hope, fought as never before. The warriors soon began to retreat after many of them were killed. Girty disappeared, the Shawnee chief lay dead, and the British had long since pulled out. The following morning, as the Native Americans were planning what to do next, **reinforcements** of 70 men finally arrived to help the fort's defenders. Peace and quiet now reigned once more at Fort Henry.

Soon more settlers, pioneers from Virginia, arrived and the settlement grew. Isaac Zane did marry the Huron princess, but he returned often to visit his family, and a treaty of peace was signed between the settlers and the Huron tribe. Colonel Ebenezer Zane opened a trading post and became the friend of Native Americans. He had a **reputation** for honest and kind dealings with all.

Betty married the **valiant** Alfred Clarke, who saved her brother. The West Virginia branch of the Daughters of the American Revolution reports that Betty and Alfred lived happily. They had several children and settled in the neighborhood of Fort Henry. The story lives on about how Elizabeth Zane saved the fort and the lives of those who afterward helped build the great city of Wheeling, West Virginia.

reinforcements: Extra soldiers

reputation: Good name

valiant: Brave

Davy Crockett – The Fearless Frontiersman

1786–1836	Tennessee–Texas

"The West" back in the late 1700s meant any land west of the original 13 colonies. Colonists looking for land to farm began to head out west with their families, hoping to acquire property and build homes. By 1800, some 400,000 homesteaders had traveled to Kentucky and Tennessee and settled there.

Who Was Davy Crockett?

Davy Crockett was born on the Nolichucky River in Greene County, Tennessee, the fifth of eight children born to John and Rebecca Crockett. Like most pioneer families, the Crocketts lived in a one-room cabin with dirt floors and just a few windows for light. They did their best to make a living, working hard all day and into the night to provide for their family. Life on the frontier was harsh, extremely dependent on the weather for growing good crops. Davy and his brothers and sisters were expected to work and help support the family.

Hired Out

When Davy was only 12 years old, a Dutchman named Jacob Siler, who worked driving cattle to market, stopped to talk to Davy's father. He had a herd of cattle and many miles left to go. He was having a hard time managing them alone.

He had watched Davy and was impressed with his **agility** and cheerfulness. He offered to pay Mr. Crockett if Davy would help him deliver this herd. Mr. Siler promised to send Davy home after they unloaded the cattle in Virginia. Mr. Crockett needed the money, so he agreed. Before Davy left, his mom Rebecca made him a new **coonskin cap**, and his father gave him a rifle.

Davy was thrilled to have his own gun to help shoot game to eat along the way. Davy's father assured him he was only **obligated** to help Mr. Siler get the cattle delivered. Then he could look for someone headed back toward home and join them. Davy watered and fed the animals and helped to keep them moving. The trip took two weeks. Mr. Siler paid Davy six dollars but then told him he had to stay to help him on his farm. Mr. Siler told him his father had changed his mind. He kept Davy very busy, but Davy wanted to go home. He was sure his father had told him he could leave after the cattle reached the market.

agility: Skillfulness

coonskin cap: A hat made from the skin and fur of a raccoon

obligated: Committed

Home Again

One day, three wagons passed Mr. Siler's home. Davy spotted Mr. Dunn, a neighbor he knew from Tennessee. Davy motioned the wagon to stop, climbed up, and explained his **dilemma**. Mr. Dunn told him he was welcome to go back to Tennessee with him. He was spending the night at the inn but planned to leave at daybreak. Davy went back to the Silers, had supper, and went to bed early. As soon as he knew the family was asleep, he gathered his things and crept quietly outside. It was snowing heavily, and the walk to town was exhausting. The snow was almost up to his knees, but he was determined to be there by daybreak. He made it. At last, he was going home!

dilemma: Problem

Time for School

Davy was so excited to finally be home. He found out that a man named Benjamin Kitchen had moved there and started a school. John Crockett had enrolled all his children, and Davy was to go also. He was the biggest boy who had not yet learned how to read. At first, Davy was enjoying school, but there was one boy, Johnny, who teased Davy when he was struggling to learn to read. Davy confronted the boy on the way home from school, and a fight began. Both boys were bruised when the fight ended, but Johnny looked a bit worse. Davy was afraid he would get a whipping from the teacher. He decided not to go to school. He just stayed in the woods during school hours.

After four days, the teacher contacted his father to ask why Davy was not in school. Mr. Crockett was angry and had a **hickory stick** waiting for Davy when he got home. Davy took off running. He was afraid to go home for he knew he'd get a whipping. He remembered another neighbor was heading for Virginia to take cattle there the next day and offered to join him. He was paid four dollars at the end of the trip. He decided to stay in Virginia for a while and work until his father's temper cooled off. He did odd jobs and time passed. It was four whole years until, just before his 16th birthday, he was so homesick he had to go home.

hickory stick: A stick used to deliver a spanking

The whole family seemed happy to have Davy home again. His father told him that he had become **indebted** to a neighbor for $35.

indebted: Something borrowed that has to be repaid

He asked if Davy would work for the neighbor for six months to pay off his debt. Davy gladly helped to pay his father's debt. He earned a reputation for being a hard worker who was honest in his dealings. He then discovered his father owed $40 to another neighbor. Without telling his father, he worked another six months to pay off that debt, as well. When Davy told his father he had paid all his debts, there were tears in his father's eyes. He told Davy he was proud of the man he had become. Not having had much schooling, Davy had a desire to learn. He found a man who would teach him if he worked for him two days a week. Davy agreed and learned quickly.

Davy Marries

Davy met a pretty, blue-eyed Irish girl named Mary Finley, who went by the name of Polly. Years later, Davy wrote in his autobiography: "He was well pleased with her from the word go."[26] They were married in August 1806. For wedding gifts, they received two cows and calves and a spinning wheel. They rented a little farm. Davy worked hard at farming, but he especially loved hunting and supplied his family with plenty of good meat. Davy's favorite game to hunt was bear. He called his trusty old rife "Old Betsy." He rarely missed a shot.

Davy and Polly had two sons, John and William. The town was growing, and more folks were moving there. For six years, Davy and Polly struggled to make ends meet. Finally, Davy, now 25 years old, figured it was time to move to western Tennessee. The government was offering land to people if they promised just to pay the taxes and fees on it.

Davy acquired a plot of land 150 miles west of Knoxville, Tennessee. The land was good for farming and hunting. In his autobiography Davy wrote, "It was here that I began to distinguish myself as a hunter and to lay the foundation for all my future greatness."[27] Davy was skillful at hunting bear, which provided the family not only with meat, but oil, fur rugs, and clothes. The population of settlers continued to grow, and in a couple of years, Davy moved his family again, close to northern Alabama.

War with the Red Sticks

The War of 1812 brought new challenges to the frontier. Many Native Americans sided with the British. One group of Native Peoples called the **Red Sticks** wanted to fight the settlers and keep them from coming west. Another group called the Lower Creek liked the ways of the settlers and had started building schools, creating farms, and herding cattle. Davy sided with the Lower Creek people to fight the Red Sticks. The Red Sticks had attacked Fort Mims on the lower part of the Alabama River and killed hundreds of men, women, and children. The Red Sticks began moving north and Davy

Red Sticks: Named for their red-painted war clubs

thought it was only time until they attacked Davy and Polly's snug little home which was a few miles north of the Alabama line. He felt it was his duty to fight, although Polly begged him not to go. He stocked up the woodpile for his family. He had plenty of meat stored as well to last them until he returned.

On September 24, 1813, he signed up with the Tennessee Volunteer Mounted Riflemen. Men volunteered for three-month terms, then returned to their farms and homes. During the harsh winter, Davy used his own money to buy blankets for the other soldiers. He also went hunting to provide the men with fresh meat. Davy was popular with the men. He entertained them by telling jokes and stories.

Davy was assigned to a scouting party. The scouts' job was to find out where Native People were and what they were doing. They had to learn to move quietly and swiftly through the woods. One night while scouting, Davy and his friend saw some of the Red Sticks hiding their canoes and then sneaking through the woods to attack sleeping soldiers. Davy sent his friend to warn the men in camp while he moved the hidden canoes. Davy waited until the Native Americans were just about ready to attack,

then hollered a terrifying yell. All the soldiers joined in. The Red Sticks were frightened and fled to the river, only to find their canoes gone. Davy and the men kept up the terrible yells. The Red Sticks were so terrified they wildly jumped into the river to escape.

Davy fulfilled his three-month term and headed home. Sometime later, a little girl was born to Davy and Polly. Sadly, six months afterward, following a brief illness Polly died. Davy wrote, "I met with the hardest trial which ever falls to the lot of man."[28] He missed his beloved Polly.

Not long after Polly's death, Davy married Elizabeth Patton, a widow with two children of her own. Her husband had been killed in the war with the Red Sticks. More people were beginning to settle in the area and Davy moved his family again to Lawrence County, 80 miles away. He opened two mills. One was a powder mill where he made gunpowder. The other mill was a grist mill where grain was ground into flour. Things were going well for Davy and his growing family, and they were happy.

Running for Office

Each county had its own company of militia which was called upon if there were an emergency. Davy was elected **colonel** of the militia in 1818. He later was elected **justice of the peace**. People liked and trusted him. He was honest and dependable — just one of the common people. He always wore his coonskin cap, and a deerskin jacket and pants. People loved his funny stories. Some were true and some were made up tales meant to make people laugh.

colonel: An officer of high rank

justice of the peace: A person appointed to act as judge

assemblyman: Member of a committee that makes laws

In February of 1821, he ran for and was elected to the office of Tennessee **assemblyman**. Colonel Crockett remarked to his wife, "I don't know why they chose me. I don't know any more about making laws than a coon dog knows about cooking."[29] Elizabeth laughed and said, "You'll learn because you are honest and fair and unafraid." His motto for life was "Be sure you are right, then go ahead."[30] That is what he did. Being an assemblyman was only a part-time job, so he still had to work to provide for his family. In the state assembly, he was a strong supporter of the rights of African Americans.

Another Move

When Davy got home from the legislature, he learned a flood had swept away his mills. He was not worried, though. He scooped up one of his daughters in his arms and announced the family would move again: 150 miles west to the area of the Obion River, a waterway in northwest Tennessee.

Davy was known for his success in hunting. With buffalo, bear, and deer meat, his family was always well-supplied. Still in need of more income, however, when he was not in the legislature, Davy started making **barrel staves**. He hired men to cut down the trees and saw them into barrel staves. They would load the staves on flat, wide boats called barges and take them down the Mississippi River.

barrel staves: Narrow lengths of wood used to form barrels

Crockett Goes to Congress

The people of Tennessee loved Davy. They asked him to run for Congress. He was elected in 1827 and again in 1829. When President Andrew Jackson wanted the Native Peoples to sign a treaty giving up all their land, which would force them to move across the Mississippi River, Davy stood up for them.

"Whoever heard of that way of doing? That land belongs to the Indians. I'll fight to help them keep it. I'll fight it with every breath in my body."[31] His friends warned him that he would not get elected again if he opposed this bill. But Davy was **adamant**. "Then I'll go home and hunt bear! I'd rather be an old coon dog belonging to a poor man in the forest than do what I know is wrong. I'll fight now for what I know is right no matter what it costs me."[32] Davy worked hard to keep the Native Americans from being moved, but Congress passed the bill anyway. Davy had spoken up for what he knew was right. He was not re-elected to Congress this time.

adamant: Unshakable in his position

The Alamo

Davy decided he was done with politics. Besides, it was getting too crowded again for him where he lived. He was going to explore westward. Texas was part of Mexico at that time, but Mexico had granted land to 30,000 Americans. Davy made up his mind to settle in the Red River Valley. This is the second-largest river basin in the Texas Panhandle. There fields were rich and green, and water was clear and sparkling. He wrote to his daughter, "Texas is the garden spot of the world. It has the best land and prospects for health I ever saw. It's worth a fortune to any man to come here. There is a world of country to settle."[33]

Trouble was brewing between Mexico and the American settlers, however. The Texans wanted their independence from Mexico. Davy took the **oath of allegiance** to the Texan government and joined the militia. President Santa Anna of Mexico decided to punish the Texans. He marched 3,000 soldiers toward San Antonio, Texas. The Alamo, an old Spanish mission, was located there. A little band of Texans was using it as a fort, holding out against the Mexican army.

Colonel **Jim Bowie** went to help the Texans. Davy went too. They arrived in February 1836. Colonel **William Travis** was in command of the small **garrison** defending the Alamo. The Mexicans attacked. Davy was skillful in hitting his targets with trusty "Old Betsy." The heroic men in the Alamo were courageous and determined, but badly outnumbered.

oath of allegiance: Promise of loyalty

Jim Bowie: A pioneer and soldier

William Travis: The lieutenant colonel of the cavalry for the Texan army

garrison: A military post

They ran out of ammunition. Santa Anna and his men came with **bayonets** ready.

Davy Crockett, Jim Bowie, and the others defended the Alamo fearlessly, but before long all lay dead. They had not died in vain, however, because their sacrifice inspired others with the words "Remember the Alamo!" This became the battle cry that empowered and united the Texans. More volunteers were inspired to join the army, ultimately leading to the decisive victory for the Texan forces at the Battle of San Jacinto on April 21, 1836. Santa Anna was taken prisoner, and Texas won its independence.

bayonets: Blades attached to the muzzle of a rifle

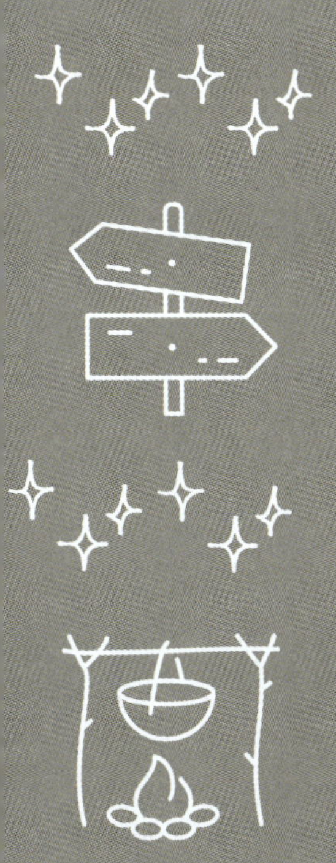

5

Jed Smith – Trapper, Hunter, and Trailblazer

1799–1831	New York–Mexico

Who Was Jed Smith?

Jedediah Strong Smith was born on January 6, 1799, in Jericho, New York. Jed's father owned a store in this small farming town. Jed loved to roam the woods and fields with his rifle. He also helped his father in the store selling supplies to townsfolk as well as to the many hunters who stopped by on their way westward. Jed loved to hear the stories they would tell of life in the West. He helped his brothers raise their family's vegetables and milk the cows. He split wood for the family, carried water, and helped with all the chores that needed to be done.

Jed's mother taught her children to read the family Bible, a practice Jed continued throughout his life. Occasionally a schoolteacher came around for a month or two to give the children lessons. Every month a Methodist preacher came to town. He liked Jed and would loan him history and geography books to read.

Moving

When Jed was 12 years old, his family moved to North East Township in Erie County, Pennsylvania. Here Jed developed a close relationship with the town doctor, Dr. Titus Simmons. Dr. Simmons often lent Jed books, and they had long talks together. He got Jed excited about his dream of going west. "Jedediah's letters are never so glowing as when they speak of the old doctor," wrote a friend.[34]

Dr. Simmons gave Jed a copy of a book published in 1814 about the Lewis and Clark Expedition to the Pacific. Jed carried this book with him on all his travels for the rest of his life. When he finished reading the book, Jed went to see Dr. Simmons. "I've looked on the map showing where they went. What about the country south of the Columbia River? There's nothing but white space on the map."[35] Dr. Simmons told him the space was white because no one knew what was there. Jed determined that he wanted to find out.

Moving Again

A few years later, Jed's family moved farther west to Green Township, Ohio, near Lake Erie. Jed was now 18 years old, strong, and tall. He was hired as an office clerk on a Lake Erie **freight** boat. British fur traders frequently hired this boat, and they liked Jed. He often helped them by writing letters for them or adding up columns of numbers they

freight: A vessel carrying goods

were working with. They told Jed of opportunities to make good money selling beaver furs. Jed asked them about the land south of the Columbia River. No one knew much.

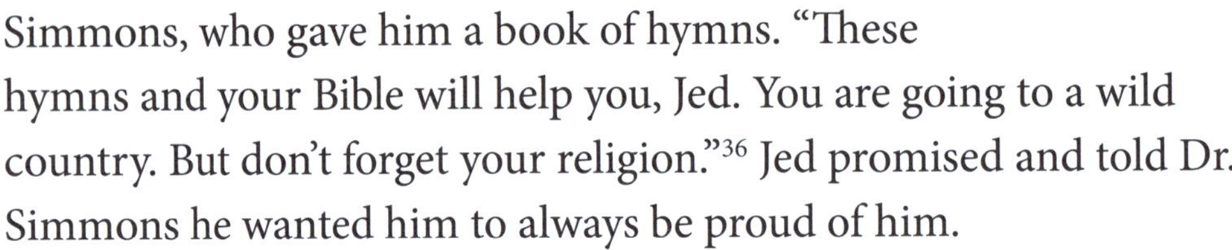

When Jed was 22 years old, he decided to go west. He planned to trap beaver and send his earnings back home to be used to help pay for his five younger brothers' education. He wanted to know what land was like in the "white space" of that map. He bade farewell to Dr. Simmons, who gave him a book of hymns. "These hymns and your Bible will help you, Jed. You are going to a wild country. But don't forget your religion."[36] Jed promised and told Dr. Simmons he wanted him to always be proud of him.

To The West

Jed made his way to Northern Illinois. He went to see a man named General William Ashley, a famous fur trader who was organizing an expedition. General Ashley was impressed with the 23-year-old young man. He hired Jed to trap for him, and on May 8, 1822, Jed joined a party of more than 100 trappers headed up the Missouri River from St. Louis. His dream was coming true at last.

The **keelboat** Jed was riding was loaded with supplies for the trappers, as well as gifts to trade with the Native Peoples. At times, the boat would stop, and Jed and a couple of other trappers would get out to hunt

keelboat: A long, narrow boat with pointed ends

for meat. Jed was a sure shot; he killed many an elk. Five months later, they arrived at a fort on the Yellowstone River. Jed set out from there with a trapping party into the Big Horn Mountains, which were a 150-mile mountain range in north central Wyoming and south-central Montana. Older and more experienced trappers taught Jed all he needed to know. He learned the best locations to set traps and how to not leave scent behind that would scare the beavers away. Jed's first beaver weighed 40 pounds. He soon had many **pelts** to sell.

At the end of autumn, Jed and the men began to build cabins to wait out the long, cold winter. The trappers commented that Jim was different from the others. He enjoyed reading books, which he did every evening. Jed would chop a hole in the ice and climb in the water to get a bath. He wanted to be clean, and he shaved each day. He was always reading his Bible and praying. Despite the differences, the other trappers really liked Jed.

pelts: Animal skins

Trouble

When spring came, Native American warriors raided the trappers' fort. Many horses were stolen. Jed was chosen to go with General Ashley to try to buy their horses back from some warriors of the Rees tribe. At first,

they seemed friendly, but as **negotiations** went on, they would only accept ammunition in exchange for horses. By evening, the trappers had traded for 19 horses. Jim feared that the warriors would decide to use that ammunition to attack them.

Since it was nighttime, they had to keep the horses on the riverbank before taking them to the fort the next day. That day, however, there was a storm; the men could not leave. They stayed awake all that night, guarding the horses. Suddenly, they heard an owl hoot. Seconds later, another owl hooted. They realized this was not a real owl, but a signal. The Rees began shooting, and the frightened horses ran away. Jed and his men ran to the river and headed for their keelboats. They lost all the horses but escaped with their lives. From then on, they tried to trade with the friendlier Crow tribes.

negotiations: Discussions meant to reach an agreement

Each summer, the trappers met at a certain location to sell their furs and purchase supplies for the next trapping season. Ashley announced that Jed Smith had earned the right to lead a trapping party. All the men congratulated Jed. Many men wanted to be under his leadership.

Fight with a Grizzly

Jed was leading his trappers one day when suddenly, someone shouted, "Grizzly! Grizzly!" A massive grizzly leaped upon Jed, who only had time to grab for his knife. Jed felt a sharp, stinging pain in his side as he plunged the knife into the grizzly. The bear tore at the top of Jed's head, but Jed kept on swinging his knife. Jed heard the crack of a rifle and one of his men telling him he had shot the bear. The bear had made a huge slice in his head and almost ripped off his ear.

When Jed tried to sit up, he was so weak his men had to help him. One of the men, Jim, grabbed a needle and thread and began sewing Jed's wounds. Jed gritted his teeth and clenched his fists, trying to stand the pain. Jim found that several of Jed's ribs were broken as well. He got Jed sewed and cleaned up and wrapped a piece of buckskin around Jed's body. "Jed," said Jim, "if that grizzly's paw hadn't hit your bullet pouch, you'd be dead."[37]

"I guess the good Lord is looking after me. I must thank Him in my prayers," said Jed weakly.[38]

That night, as he lay by the campfire, Jed read his Bible, said his prayers, and rolled up in his blanket. One of the men, Dave Jackson, remarked, "Jed is a strange one with his Bible reading and praying. I've never seen another man like him in this country. But he is a MAN!"[39]

Winter in Camp

The trapping party spent the winter of 1824 in a Crow camp in the Rocky Mountains. The friendly community in the camp were glad to have company. It was a cold, windy winter, and snow piled up. The Crows called the Rockies the "Shining Mountains." They talked about a path that led through the mountains. Jed wanted to find it. He set out in February from the Crow camp to look for it, although it was still terribly cold and windy. Jed and his men traveled through what is now southern Wyoming.

Soon the food supply began to **dwindle**. The hunting was sparse, the streams were frozen solid. The men had to melt snow to get water to drink. Finally, the exhausted men reached a wide opening in the mountains. They were elated to realize they had found the pass! Jed had found the one place where wagons could cross the Rockies. In the years to come, thousands of settlers would use this South Pass to go to California and Oregon.

dwindle: Get low

Beaver were plentiful on the western side of the Rockies. In just a month, the men had so many furs that they had to send three men to deliver them to General Ashley. Jed, meanwhile, took the rest of the men northwest to explore the new beaver country.

Jed Buys the Fur Company

In the summer of 1827, General Ashley told Jed he was going to **retire** and asked Jed and two other men if they wanted to buy his fur business. The three men accepted. They decided Jed would explore new beaver territory, and Dave Jackson and Bill Sublette would lead trapping parties. Jed studied his maps again, wanting to explore the "white space" southwest of Great Salt Lake.

retire: Leave his job

He left with 17 men and rode through the barren, dry hills. As the days dragged on, they found many rivers had run dry. The horses and mules would die if they didn't find water and grass soon. Some of the men begged Jed to turn back. Jed promised them they would reach a **Mojave** village soon. The men **marveled** when the settlement came into sight. One of his men said, "Jed has a feeling for the country. Those eyes of his seem to see through mountains."[40] The kindly Mojaves fed the starving trappers and traded horses to them for beads and cloth.

Mojave: Native American tribe

marveled: Were filled with astonishment

After resting, Jed and his men started to go west through the Mojave Desert. It was almost unbearable, even hotter and drier than what they'd already passed through. They were soon in California. At that time, California was still owned by Mexico.

From the desert, they then went through the San Bernardino Mountains. The men were so exhausted they kept stumbling and falling down. Finally, they reached the top! Reaching a green valley with sparkling clear water, Jed knelt and gave thanks to God for helping him get his men to safety.

California

Jed went to see the governor of California, but the governor was not happy to see Jed. He feared that the Americans might be planning to take California from Mexico. Jed explained that he and his men were only trappers and wanted to buy supplies and head home. The Governor agreed to sell them supplies but told them they had to go back the way they had come. He was trying to keep Jed from seeing any more of California's rich lands. The trappers started east but Jed decided not to risk his men's lives anymore crossing the desert. "I think the Lord will forgive me for disobeying the governor," he told his men.[41]

Before long, they entered the San Joaquin Valley. It was teeming with deer, bear, and beaver. The men soon had many pelts. On May 20, they started east again, looking for a pass through the mountains. There was still snow from four to eight feet deep. The winds were blowing wildly. It looked like it would be impossible to find a pass. High cliffs seemed to block the way. Three times in one day, they had to turn around. On the fourth try, they found a pass at last! Jeb and his men were the first white men to cross the Sierra Nevada Mountains. The trip had taken only eight days!

Nevada

The next challenge would be more desert — in Nevada. They pressed on, even though their eyes ached, and their throats were **parched** with thirst. Two of the men could barely walk by the time they reached the Great Salt Desert in Utah. Jed urged them on. He writes in his journal, "June 24 — I started very early in hopes of soon finding water. But ascending a high point I could discover nothing but sandy plains. When I came down, I durst not tell my men of the desolate prospect ahead, but framed my story so as to discourage them as little as possible."[42]

parched: Dry

One of the men named Robert soon fell to his

knees saying he could not go on. Jed buried him in the sand up to his neck so he would have protection from the baking sun and set out to find water. In only a few miles, they miraculously came upon a flowing spring! The men drank and brought water back to Robert. Jed writes in his journal, "I have observed that a man reduced by hunger is some days in recovering his strength. A man equally reduced by thirst seems renovated almost instantly."[43] Such was the case with Robert, who was soon able to travel on to the spring himself after drinking.

They all rested by the spring for a day before setting out again. It took eight more days to reach Bear Lake, where they were to meet the other trappers. It was amazing! They had actually done what no other American had ever done. They had crossed the Great Salt Lake Desert.

Jed continued to trap and explore for the next few years. He reached St. Louis in October 1830, after his last year of trapping. It had been a good one. He and his two friends had sold their fur trading business. Jed wanted to settle down and farm. He was able to help his parents and brothers financially. He also sent gifts to his good friend, Dr. Simmons. He made a substantial donation to the St. Louis church. Jed began working on his own map of the Far West. He was also writing a book to tell others about the incredible land west of the Mississippi. Jed Smith had indeed managed to fill in the white spaces on the map!

6

Lewis and Clark – Expedition to the West

1804–1806	From Missouri to the Pacific and Back

When Thomas Jefferson was President of the United States in 1801, the country was made up of 17 states. It extended only as far west as the Mississippi River. In 1803, he acquired about 828,000 square miles of land for $15,000,000. This became known as the Louisiana Purchase. In time, 14 more states would be added to the nation from this land purchase. President Jefferson believed that the future of the United States lay in the West. He sent a highly experienced party of explorers to discover all they could about the vast new territory.

Who Were Lewis and Clark?

Meriwether Lewis was born in Albemarle County, Virginia, on August 18, 1774. Jefferson had known Lewis from the time of his birth. After serving in the army, Lewis became Jefferson's secretary and was honored when Jefferson chose him to lead the **Corps of Discovery**. Lewis was well-suited for the job. He loved the outdoors and was skillful in hunting, fishing, and navigating in the woods. Jefferson let Lewis choose another officer: "If Lewis were killed by a grizzly bear (as he nearly was) or shot by Indians (he once actually felt the wind of a Native American's bullet, whizzing above his head) or stomped to death by a buffalo bull (a big one just missed

Corps of Discovery: An expedition exploring the Louisiana Purchase

trampling him in his tent one night), or bitten by a rattlesnake (another near-tragedy), there would have to be someone else to assume command at once."[44]

Lewis at once decided to ask his friend, First Lieutenant William Clark, under whom Lewis had served as a second lieutenant in a rifle company. He knew Clark to be a brave, resourceful woodsman with much experience in the wilderness. Clark also had the skill of being able to draw maps, which would prove invaluable. President Jefferson approved his choice, as he had known the Clark family for years. When asked to join the expedition, Clark responded, "My friend, I join you with hand and heart."[45]

Although the two men had very different personalities, they complimented one another; no one ever heard them have a disagreement. They carefully chose men to accompany them who were good hunters, skilled woodsmen, and hard workers. One of the men they selected was an experienced river pilot, and another was an expert in Native American languages.

Lewis began collecting supplies. Congress granted them $2,500 to outfit the expedition. They purchased rifles, ammunition, clothing, gifts for the Native Americans they may encounter, and even a collapsible boat he had designed. They included a swivel gun — a small cannon that could be moved to fire either from a boat or a fort. They packed almost 200 pounds of dried, **condensed** soup, 3,400 pounds of flour, 50 kegs of pork, 560 pounds of biscuits, and 750 pounds of salt. They also brought coffee, peas, beans, **lard**, sugar, and candles. Pots, axes, drills, and files were part of the equipment, along with medicines.

The explorers were instructed to keep careful records and maps. They were to write in their journals daily, describing everything they saw, including plants, animals, and minerals. Lewis decided to take his large, faithful Newfoundland dog Seaman along on the journey. Captain Lewis had paid $20 for him, which was a considerable amount for a dog. Seaman accompanied the men all the way to the Pacific Ocean and back again.

The expedition set out from St. Louis, where the Mississippi and Missouri Rivers meet. Neither man knew what to expect but they were ready to find out. At 4 p.m. on May 14, 1804, citizens lined up to cheer them off with well wishes. After they set out, Seaman would often leap out of the boat to grab squirrels swimming down the river. He dutifully provided the crew with much meat doing that. He proved to be a great **asset** in many ways.

condensed: A thick stock to which you add water

lard: Fat used in cooking

asset: Valuable

Off for the West

They soon discovered that traveling on the river was not going to be easy. Both **sandbars** and **rapids** slowed them down occasionally. Floating logs were hazardous. The journey was not made any easier by continual pelting rain. The heat was intense, and mosquito bites made everyone miserable, including poor Seaman.

From July through November, they met up with various Native American tribes, most of whom were friendly. By winter, they had traveled 1,600 miles, but there were still 1,000 miles to go. Snow began to fall. The Missouri River froze over. It was time to settle in for the winter.

sandbars: Areas of shallow sand in the water

rapids: Dangerously fast-flowing waters

The explorers began to build a fort close to what is now Bismarck, North Dakota, where 4,400 friendly Mandan Native Americans made their home. They named it Fort Mandan after the peaceable tribe. The winter of 1804–1805 saw temperatures reach 40 degrees below zero. Herds of buffalo roamed the Missouri River without breaking through the ice. The Corps of Discovery was joined that winter by a fur trader named Toussaint Charbonneau

and his wife Sacagawea, a member of the Shoshone tribe. They both knew Native languages and agreed to travel with the group.

Spring Arrives with New Dangers

Now the team was headed for **uncharted** territory, and new challenges awaited. They were coming to places not even many Native Americans had hunted. One day, they counted 220 grizzly bears. Several of the men, Captain Lewis included, barely escaped death before they learned how to handle this new challenge. Sometimes, the animals required as many as ten bullets to kill them, they were so enormous. If a bear was shot but not killed, it would attack savagely. Men hunting grizzlies had to go out in large parties to protect each other.

uncharted: Unfamiliar

Tremendous prairie rattlesnakes, sometimes as much as four feet long, were another real danger. One night, a huge buffalo charged through the camp, barely missing the tent the captains shared. Seaman chased it off by barking ferociously. The explorers decided to make a **cache** in which to hide some of their supplies. They planned to pick them up on the return journey.

cache: A pit dug in the ground

On June 10, 1805, Lewis and four other men heard a thunderous rush of water. It was coming from The Great Falls, still seven miles away. This is where the Missouri River tumbled down into five different waterfalls, all in a row. Some of the falls dropped as much as 600 feet. Captain Lewis wrote in his journal that the Great Falls "were the grandest sight I ever beheld."[46] Clark and the others arrived six days later.

Although the falls were magnificent, the steep climb to cross them was going to be difficult. They would have to carry all the supplies up steep paths to **circumvent** the falls. It took 11 days to make the 18-mile hike. **Pear cactus** thorns along the path made everyone's feet bruised and bloody. They were pounded not only with driving rain, but hail. They had to be on the lookout for rattlesnakes lodged in the rocks, and of course, grizzlies were plentiful. Clark helped to save Charbonneau and Sacagawea from a **flash flood**.

circumvent: Go around

Pear cactus: A prickly plant

flash flood: A sudden flood due to heavy rainfall

Horses

At last, Sacagawea recognized that they were close to where she had been kidnapped many years ago close to her village. Soon they found her tribe, and Sacagawea was reunited with her brother, who was now chief of the tribe. Sacagawea **translated** for Lewis and Clark, and they traded with the Shoshones for 29 horses and a mule. Now, at last, they could cross the Rocky Mountains! Again, they buried supplies to retrieve later.

Sacagawea's brother ordered a man, "Old Toby," to lead them over the rough Rockies. Crossing the Lolo Trail, which is a pass through the Bitterroot Mountains along the present-day Idaho-Montana border, was one of the worst experiences of the entire journey. The landscape was wild and the men were exhausted. It grew colder. Their only water was melted snow. Clark wrote, "We are continually covered with snow. I have been wet and as cold in every part as I ever was in my life, indeed I was at one time fearful my feet would freeze in the thin **Mockirsons** which I wore."[47]

translated: Interpreted

Their food supply dwindled. They ate wolf, crayfish, and even candles (made from fat) to stay alive. Some horses lost their footing and rolled down a slippery slope. Finally, the days of starvation were over. They had survived the toughest part of the trail. Hunters brought in four deer and some salmon.

Mockirsons: Clark's spelling of moccasins

Clark went ahead of the others to set up a camp. Lewis and some of his men were so exhausted they had to lie across their horses' backs. Almost all Lewis' men were ill. They had to take a bit of time to recover their strength before pressing on to the last leg of the long journey. When everyone was better, they began to make canoes from fallen trees to make the last leg on the Clearwater River. The Nez Perce people were friendly and offered to keep their horses until they returned. Their chiefs even accompanied them for some miles. Soon the explorers began to meet Native People who knew a bit of English.

There were two more danger points to overcome. The entire current of the mighty Columbia River rushes between narrow rock walls at Short Narrows. They relied on their expert riverman to guide them through the swiftly moving waters. By early November, they came upon the giant trees in the Oregon forests. They observed many **cascades** of falling water. It was beautiful, but hard to keep dry. Dry firewood was almost impossible to find, and the men were often cold.

Ocean

Finally, one day, Clark hollered, "Ocean, ocean in view!" They had fought their way across the continent and

cascades: Small waterfalls

reached the mighty Pacific Ocean. The continent could be crossed, after all! The explorers set to building a fort and winter camp. By Christmas 1805, they were all comfortably settled in their new cabins with big fireplaces to keep warm. They named their new headquarters Fort Clatsop after the friendly Clatsop tribe who lived nearby. The Corps of Discovery had earned a well-deserved rest. Clark spent the winter drawing maps, and the men hunted for game.

Long Road Home

On March 23, 1806, they set out for home. They had been away almost two years and were anxious to return. They had many challenges on their return trip. The Columbia River was extremely high and dangerous. Sacagawea's little boy got sick. Clark gave him some of the medicine he had brought, and it cured him. Word spread through the tribes that Clark could heal the sick. They lined up to be treated, and Clark did have success in many cases by employing wise treatments. A late May snow blocked the route through the Rocky Mountains. They had to turn back to give it time to melt. By June 29, they reached the Lolo Trail's hot bubbling springs. Everyone rested their sore muscles and tired backs in the comforting springs.

On July 3, Lewis and Clark split up the Corps to explore. Lewis took Seaman and nine men on horseback on a route that followed alongside the Missouri River. Clark, Sacagawea, Charbonneau, and 18 other men with 40 horses headed south for the Yellowstone River. Sacagawea led Clark's group to the Shoshone country. There they dug up the canoes, food, and supplies they had buried.

Clark's party was soon on the Jefferson River. Half the men canoed and half rode horses. They reached Three Forks of the Missouri where the three rivers converge to form the Missouri River on July 13. Clark, Sacagawea, Charbonneau, and eight other men were to ride down to the Yellowstone River with their 49 horses. The remaining 10 men would canoe down to meet Lewis and his men. On July 25, Clark came to a high **sandstone bluff**. It was about 150 feet high. Clark carved his name and July 25, 1806, on it, and it became a National Historic Landmark.

sandstone bluff: A steep shoreline slope formed of rock made of quartz sand

Lewis was to meet Clark where the Yellowstone River met the Missouri River. When Clark arrived, Lewis wasn't there. However, many biting mosquitoes were. Clark left Lewis a note telling him they'd meet farther down the Missouri River at Great Falls. He had to get away from those mosquitoes.

On August 11, Lewis and his men met up with Clark. They had been separated for 40 days and were so thankful to be together again. It was a joyous reunion. On September 23, 1806, the two captains and their men arrived at the camp near St. Louis. They were regarded as heroes, especially since most Americans thought they were dead. Clark praised Sacagawea for all her help. He wrote to Charbonneau that his wife "deserved a greater reward for her attention and services on that route than we had in our power to give her."[48]

Meeting Jefferson

Lewis and Clark shared much knowledge with President Jefferson. They told him about more than 200 plants thus far unknown, and more than 120 animals, previously unknown, including bison, bighorn sheep, porcupines, coyotes, and woodpeckers. They also learned valuable information from the friendly Native American tribes. In 28 months, they had traveled over 8,000 miles in the wilderness. Thousands of pioneer families set out for the West in the months afterward, using maps provided by Lewis and Clark. Jefferson praised them: "Never did a similar event excite more joy through the United States."[49] The Lewis and Clark Expedition did much to open up the lands of the West to all Americans.

* A map of the Lewis and Clark Expedition can by found at the end of Chapter 7.

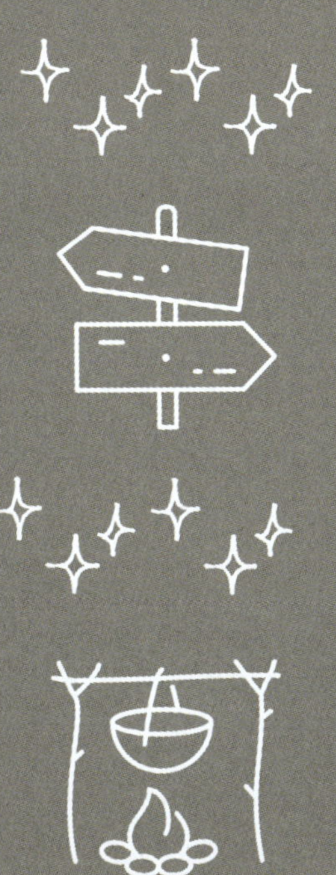

7

John Colter – The Race for Life

1808	Jefferson River, near Missouri's Headwaters

Who Was John Colter?

A baby boy was born to Joseph and Ellen Colter in Augusta County, Virginia, sometime in 1775. They named him John. When John was about four years old, his family moved farther west to Limestone, now Maysville, Kentucky. John grew up as a boy on the frontier. His father taught him how to handle and shoot a gun. By the time he was 10 years old, he was one of the best shots around.

John left home when he was about 18 years old. He grew tired of farming. For 10 years, he roamed around the woods, living off nature. He made friends with Native People and learned their ways, which served him well later in life. He loved hearing stories of Daniel Boone and wanted to be like him.

When he was 29 years old, he heard that a man named William Clark, a captain in the U.S. Army, was looking for strong woodsmen to accompany him on a special mission. A friend of his told him, "He's heard about you, John Colter, and he's particularly interested in talking to you."[50] Colter thought he might as well check it out.

He knocked on Clark's door and was let in by a red-haired man who introduced himself as Captain William Clark. He was also a captain just like Captain Meriwether Lewis.

Captain Clark told John that he and Captain Lewis had been appointed by President Thomas Jefferson to **recruit** men to join them on an exploring **expedition**. "We are looking for a special breed of men, men like you, John Colter. I have watermen, men experienced in navigating rough waters. I have cooks, carpenters, a translator, and a blacksmith. But what I need now are men who can feed us, hunters who are sure shots, strong, and long-enduring."[51] These men would form a group known as the Corps of Discovery. Clark explained that Jefferson had purchased a vast amount of land west of the Mississippi River from the French, but really knew nothing of what it was like. "It would be an adventure of a lifetime," thought John, so he signed on. He set off to join Captain Lewis and the others in the Missouri Territory.

recruit: Find men to join

expedition: A journey or voyage

With Captain Clark

Captain Clark was a cheerful man, but Captain Lewis usually kept to himself. The men stayed the winter at Camp Wood by the Wood River in Illinois before starting their expedition. To fight off boredom, the men would wrestle and compete in races. John always won. John also entertained the men by telling them stories he made up.

Supplies for the trip arrived from the army **depot** at Harpers Ferry almost daily. They had a cannon, barrels of gunpowder, and metal to make musket balls. They had plenty of beads, coats, ribbon, and **looking glasses** to give as gifts to the Native People along the way, as they would surely encounter some. They also had 4,000 pounds of pork and flour, 2,000 pounds of cornmeal, 750 pounds of salt, 600 pounds of grease, and 560 pounds of biscuits.

depot: Storehouse

looking glasses: Mirrors

Captain Lewis gave each man a flannel uniform and red long johns for warmth. John reluctantly put away his buckskin clothes. A 55-foot keelboat was built to carry the men up the river and a flat-bottomed boat for carrying supplies. At last, spring arrived. On May 14, 1804, the company headed out.

Trouble with Some Native People

In late September, they ran across their first hostile tribe, the Teton Sioux. Captain Lewis gave their leader, Black Buffalo, coats and tobacco. The chief told them they could go back down the river or stay with them but could not go on upriver. The shoreline was lined with

Sioux warriors who had their arrows pointed straight at the travelers. Captain Lewis told his men to be ready to fight. Just before Lewis' men fired the cannon, Black Buffalo decided he had enough coats and tobacco and let them pass on.

Passing the Winter

Winter was approaching again. The men were near the Mandan tribe, which was friendly to settlers. They set up camp and spent the winter there, in what is now North Dakota. It was here that Toussaint Charbonneau and his wife Sacagawea came to offer their help in exchange for traveling the rest of the way with the party. Sacagawea was of the Shoshone tribe and had been kidnapped by an enemy tribe when she was 12 years old. She hadn't been home since. Sacagawea promised to appeal to her tribe to obtain horses for the men if they could meet up with them.

In February, Sacagawea gave birth to a baby boy. They set off again in the spring. After three months, Sacagawea said they were close to her tribe. She was overjoyed to see her people again as they approached the camp. Sacagawea suddenly began running

— right into the arms of her long-lost brother, Cameahwait. He was thrilled to see his sister again and gladly agreed to trade horses to the expedition. Sacagawea surprised everyone by offering to accompany the men all the way to the Pacific Ocean, the final destination, before returning to her tribe on the trip back.

The Pacific

John witnessed firsthand the crashing waves of the mighty Pacific Ocean pounding on the rocky shore. He saw things he'd never seen before, like squirrels that flew, mice that hopped, deer with ears as big as a mule's ears, and mighty herds of buffalo in vast numbers. Captain Clark carved evidence of their presence into a tall pine tree on a ledge high above the ocean. "December 3, 1805 'By land from the U. States in 1804 and 5.'"[52]

Clark set up a winter camp and called it Fort Clatsop. On March 23, 1806, they set out for home at last. They met up with two trappers who were going upriver in search of better hunting. At night by the campfire, the trappers told of their adventures. "Beaver's plentiful, and it's in big demand for hats back east. If you can keep people from stealing the **hairy bank notes** out from under you, you can get plenty of money for spring and fall ones."[53]

The more John thought about it, the less he wanted to go back to large crowds of people. The trappers invited him to stay with them. Captain Lewis told him, "There hasn't been a job mean enough or dangerous enough that I haven't counted on you to do, no questions and no complaints. We brought you in as a hunter, yet you've willingly helped us lug boats over mountain passes no goat could conquer . . . and you've faced hostiles without blinking an eye. You're as rugged and smart as any man among us. I hereby release you from the Corps of Discovery and the U.S. Army. Your pay will be waiting for you in the Bank of St. Louis whenever you're ready."[54]

hairy bank notes: Pelts worth money

John hunted during the fall of 1806 and spring of 1807 but didn't have the success he expected. Once during his wanderings, he happened upon a mud hole that was gurgling, as if it were boiling. He held out his hand and to his amazement, it was hot. He watched in awe at other boiling mud holes. Suddenly, he saw a rush of water that looked like a waterfall

moving in reverse. The water shot in the air as high as a tree. It was incredible. John was the first settler to see the geysers of Yellowstone Park! He marked a tree with an X and initialed it with "JC."

Finally, John began to feel homesick. He decided to head home. He chopped down a tree and hollowed it out to make a canoe, as he had learned from some Native People. Loading it up with his pelts, he said goodbye to his two friends and started down the Missouri River for St. Louis.

At one point, the Blackfoot tribe took John prisoner and carried him off to their village. He listened as they discussed among themselves how to put him to death. The chief approached him finally and said, "I have decided to let you race for your life. My men will beat you, unless you are able to keep them from catching you. Can you run fast?"[55] John was a good runner, but he did not want the chief to know that. He said he was a poor runner, and the warriors would most likely easily catch him, but he said, "I will do the best I can."[56]

Race for Life

The warriors led John out to the prairie, turned him loose, and with a horrific yell started the chase. Each carried a spear or **tomahawk**. Colter had no weapon, and he was barefoot. They had removed most of his clothing as well. Fear for his life drove him on. He knew the river was six miles away. Halfway there, he turned around to see that only a few of the warriors were keeping up with him. Just one was very close to him. The others were running out of steam and falling behind.

tomahawk: A single-handed ax

Colter sped on with everything in him, knowing his life was at stake. Soon he saw the one warrior only 20 yards behind him with his spear ready to throw. Colter stopped suddenly and turned. The man tried to stop but lost his balance and fell to the ground gasping for breath. Colter quickly took advantage of the situation, seized the warrior's spear, and thrust it into him, leaving him dead. He started again for the river. Now some of the others were beginning to catch up. Seeing their dead "brother" they stopped to mourn, as was their custom, and then started pursuing John again.

Colter made it to the river. He plunged in and began swimming with all his strength to a small island. The warriors, still in pursuit, reached the shore a bit later. Thinking they had caught him at last, they began yelling loudly. John, however, dove under some driftwood and came to a spot between two logs where a pile of brush had lodged. He **submerged** himself and waited, with just his eyes and nose above the water. He was hungry; every muscle in his body ached. He put one end of a hollow reed in his mouth, leaving the other end sticking out of the water. This is how he breathed for quite some time. He lay very still as the Native People darted all over the island searching. When they approached his driftwood and brush pile, he sank back under the water, holding his breath. At last the Native People left, assuming Colter had drowned.

submerged: Covered with water

The following day, Colter swam to land. He walked 200 miles on his bare and bruised feet. He had no gun or any means of **procuring** food, so he lived on roots and berries for many days. He walked during the night and rested during the day. After 12 days he came to Fort Raymond, where the Bighorn River meets the Yellowstone in present-day Montana.

procuring: Obtaining

He half stumbled and half crawled to the gate. His tongue was parched, and he couldn't shout. He could only whimper. The gates opened. Men carried John inside and gave him water. They didn't recognize him at first. The mountain men nursed the near-dead Colter back to health. He told them his amazing story.

John eventually married and settled down in Missouri. When the War of 1812 started, he joined up. He was not killed in battle but died of **jaundice**. Many people never believed his story about finding the hot springs at Yellowstone until the late 1880s when John's initials on the tree at Yellowstone Park were discovered. A peak in the southeastern part of Yellowstone National Park is named for John Colter.

jaundice: When someone's liver is not working properly

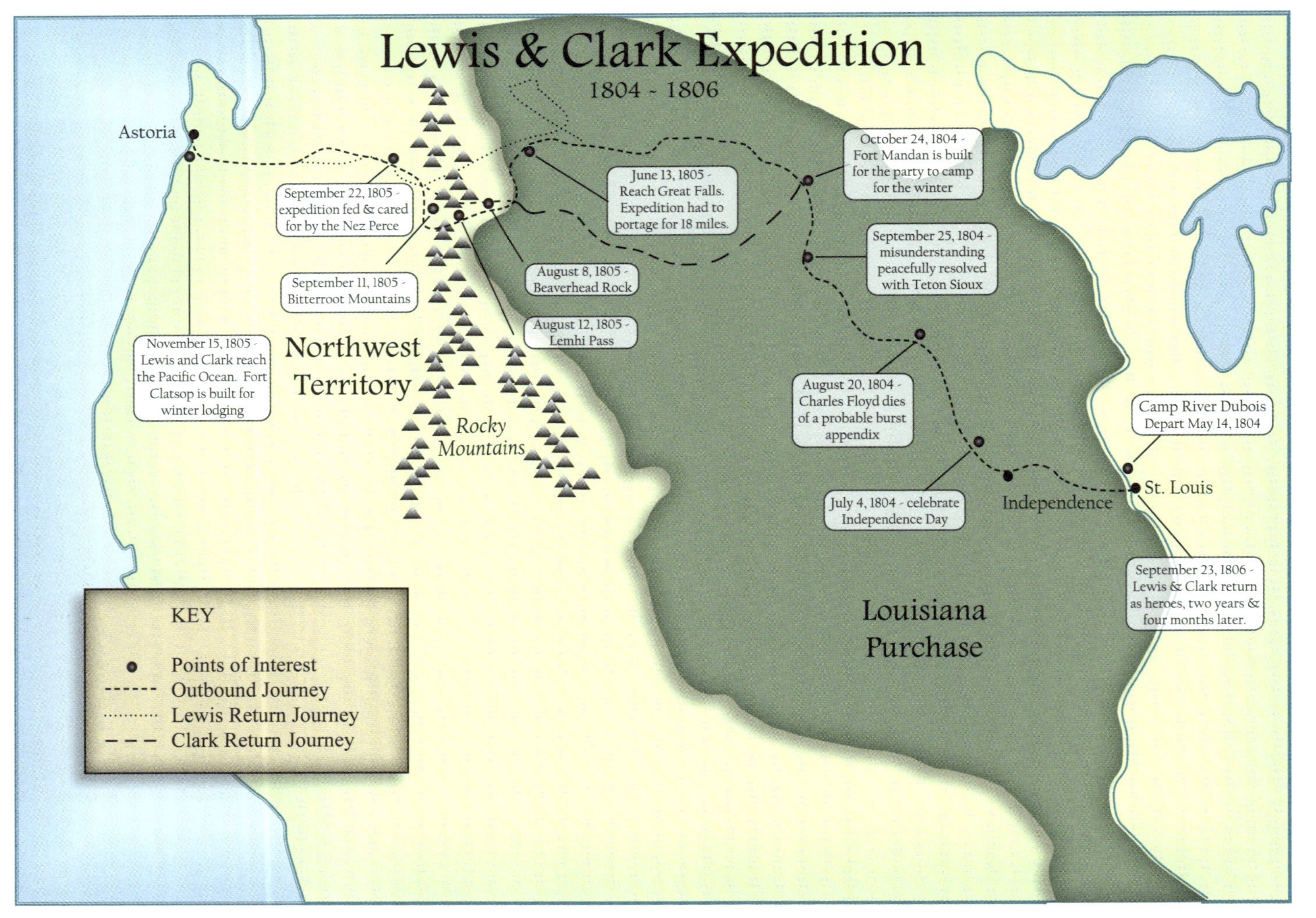
Lewis & Clark Expedition
1804 - 1806
Astoria
September 22, 1805 - expedition fed & cared for by the Nez Perce
September 11, 1805 - Bitterroot Mountains
November 15, 1805 - Lewis and Clark reach the Pacific Ocean. Fort Clatsop is built for winter lodging
Northwest Territory
Rocky Mountains
June 13, 1805 - Reach Great Falls. Expedition had to portage for 18 miles.
August 8, 1805 - Beaverhead Rock
August 12, 1805 - Lemhi Pass
October 24, 1804 - Fort Mandan is built for the party to camp for the winter
September 25, 1804 - misunderstanding peacefully resolved with Teton Sioux
August 20, 1804 - Charles Floyd dies of a probable burst appendix
July 4, 1804 - celebrate Independence Day
Independence
Camp River Dubois Depart May 14, 1804
St. Louis
September 23, 1806 - Lewis & Clark return as heroes, two years & four months later.
Louisiana Purchase
KEY
Points of Interest
Outbound Journey
Lewis Return Journey
Clark Return Journey

Kit Carson – American Trapper

1809–1868	Rocky Mountains

Who Was Kit Carson?

Christopher (Kit) Carson was born in Kentucky on Christmas Eve, 1809. His parents, Lindsay and Becky, moved to Missouri about a year later, and here Kit spent his boyhood years. He hunted and learned the ways of the woods. Kit could not read or write, but he knew the name of each tree and what it was used for. He learned the habits of all the wild animals and how best to trap them. He noticed all the animal tracks and could identify the sounds each one made. Tragically, Kit's father was killed when Kit was nine years old. He had been cutting down a large tree when a huge limb fell on him and killed him instantly.

Apprenticed

To help their struggling family earn money, Kit's mother decided to apprentice Kit to a saddlemaker, meaning Kit would learn the saddle-making craft from the expert. Kit could not stand the thought of being cooped up in a shop instead of being out in the woods. He did his best, but his heart was always outdoors with the mountain men who often stopped by the shop.

One day Captain Charles Bent, a famous fur trader, walked into the shop. Kit knew who he was; he had been watching him getting the wagon train ready. Kit asked him if he needed an extra hand. Bent wanted to know about his riding skills and whether he had a gun. Bent said he could use another cavvy boy on this trip. A cavvy boy cared for the extra mules, horses, and cattle. Kit confidently assured him he was up to the job. Bent told him to be ready to pull out at sunup. "I pay cavvy boys a dollar a day," he said. Kit was amazed. He would have paid Captain Bent for the chance to travel with him, and now Kit was going to earn a dollar a day!

During the long trip, the food supply began to dwindle. Captain Bent asked Kit to go ahead of the group and look for food. That night, he returned to the party discouraged. He had only been able to shoot and bring one wolf. Captain Bent, though, was excited. He explained to Kit, "Wolves mean buffalo. The wolf pack follows the buffalo herd. They want meat as much as we do. Let's go."[57] Captain Bent was an excellent hunter. That night the men feasted on roasted buffalo. Finally, their wagon train reached Santa Fe, New Mexico. Kit was fascinated by the town. When Captain Bent was ready to head back to Missouri, Kit was unwilling to go. Bent told Kit he was the best trail rider he'd seen in years. They bid each other goodbye.

Taos — Mountain Men Headquarters

A few **scouts** from Bent's **caravan** were going to Taos, New Mexico. Kit decided to join them. Taos was the **headquarters** for the mountain men. Kit ran into an old man he knew — Old Kincade. He used to live near the Carsons in Missouri. Old Kincade invited Kit to his hut, and there he taught him some frontier wisdom. "We got no maps out here, just memory. So you put your memory to work. Never turn a bend in a hurry. Look back and learn the lay of the land. Never leave a river in a hurry. They're all different. Learn how it tastes and looks and runs. Then you'll know when you see it again. Keep looking and learning all the time, Kit."[58]

scouts: Men sent ahead to gather information

caravan: A group of people traveling together

headquarters: Center of operations

In the spring, Old Kincade died. Kit hit the trail again, glad for his time with his old friend. Kit walked 80 miles back to Santa Fe, living on rabbits and prairie dogs. There were no jobs to be had in Santa Fe. A bit discouraged, Kit walked the 80 miles back to Taos and went directly to Young's Trading Post. He begged Captain Ewing Young to let him work for him.

Young was an experienced fur trapper and trader who had opened the trading post at Taos.

Captain Young told him he was too small. Then he asked Kit how he got there. Kit said he walked 80 miles in three days. Answering the question of what he ate, Kit told him anything he might shoot along the way. Captain Young exclaimed that Kit might be small for his age, but he certainly was tough. He told Kit he was headed north soon with 40 men to trap beaver. The people back East were all wearing tall hats made of beaver skins, and a trapper could get rich selling the skins. Kit was ready to join the men. He was 19 when he went to work for Captain Young.

Trapping Beaver

Kit, though he already knew much, soon found out there was much yet to be learned. For instance, the best time to catch a beaver is in cold weather because that is when their coats are the thickest. Yet, you must trap them before the streams freeze over. You must always be alert for signs that beavers are near. Beavers use logs to build their dams. A piece of torn-up bark or a chewed tree lets you know beavers are nearby. However, beavers can smell a man a mile away. Water is the only thing that washes away a human scent.

Traps were set in swift, cold rivers. They had to be big enough to hold a 50-pound fighting beaver trying to escape. Kit learned how to properly skin a beaver, and how to stretch the skins on sticks to dry. Captain Young taught Kit how to roast the body for eating.

Alert for Danger

Trappers must always be alert for danger. One day, while setting traps along the Salt River, Captain Young warned the men to be quiet and grab their guns. He told them to head back to camp and hide under their blankets or anything they could find. Kit ran back and crawled under his blanket, holding fast to his gun. Peeking out, he saw that the ridge was covered with Native American warriors. Young told them to hold their fire. He wanted to trick them into believing no one was there. Closer and closer they came. Captain Young yelled, "Fire!" When the attack was over, 15 of the Native People lay dead. This was Kit's first time shooting a person, and he felt sick. Captain Young comforted him and told him he knew how he felt, but in the wilderness it was either defend yourself or die.

To California

Captain Young really liked Kit. He took him along on a trip to California. It was a rough "school," as the entire party almost died of thirst while crossing the desert, and they had to defend themselves again against attack. On his way home, Kit trapped in the Rocky Mountains. There he met famous mountain men like Jim Bridger. Kit was now 22 years old. He had a horse that he bought with money he earned from his beaver pelts.

Kit heard that Captain Bent was again looking for men. Kit found him near the Arkansas River. Bent asked if Kit would like to help him build a fort. He needed a good man to head up the log-cutting crew. Kit went right to work setting up the logging camp. The work went well.

One night, two friendly Native Americans from the Cheyenne tribe visited the camp — Little Turtle and Black Whiteman. As they tied their ponies, they noticed no one was guarding the horses. In the morning, all the horses were gone; only their two little ponies were left. Sixty Crow warriors had sneaked into camp and stolen the horses. Kit was upset with himself for failing to have the horses guarded. He was determined to get his horse and the other horses back.

It seemed pretty hopeless to try to catch the warriors since they had a good head start, but the men trusted Kit and followed him. Little Turtle and Black Whiteman rode on their ponies. The men walked for two long days nonstop. On the third day, it began snowing. Walking was difficult. Suddenly, Kit pointed to smoke rising from a group of pine trees. Kit came up with a plan. He told Little Turtle and Black Whiteman to ride ahead and hide. When Kit and other men began the attack, they were to get the horses. The two friendly warriors nodded to show that they understood.

Suddenly, a dog started barking at Kit and his men. The Crow warriors came charging toward them. Kit remembered what he had learned earlier. He shouted for the men to hide, hold their fire, and not shoot until he gave the order. When the warriors were close enough to almost touch, Kit hollered, "Fire!" All the men shot at once, and three warriors fell dead. The rest of their group ran toward the pine trees, only to find the horses they had stolen were gone. Fearing for their lives, they raced off, assuming a large force was attacking them. Kit's men, including Little Turtle and Black Whiteman, began cheering Kit and shaking his hand. Kit ran over to his horse. He was so happy to have him back again.

The men rode their horses back to camp, and the two warriors returned to their Cheyenne tribe. They told their chief how Kit had outsmarted the dreaded Crows. Their chief, Yellow Wolf, listened to the report and then mounted his horse to find Kit. "I wish to see the small white leader who chased the Crows," he said.[59] He asked Kit to kneel before him. Raising his hand above Kit's head, he said, "My son, you have a brave heart. You went after your horses on foot and got them back. With few men, you beat many Crows. From this day, among my people, your name will be 'Vih'hui-nis, Little Chief of the Cheyennes.'"[60]

Encounter with Bears

Kit Carson was becoming well-known throughout the Rockies. He began leading his own expeditions; many men tried to sign up to join him. Carson only chose a few good men — he was a good judge of men. They spent one summer trapping in the **Medicine Bow Mountains**. They did well, but as winter came on, food grew scarce. One night Kit headed out into the woods to hunt elk. He was concerned for the welfare of his men. After tracking a herd of elk for several miles, he saw them grazing on a nearby hillside. He shot and killed one of them. As he ran toward it, he saw two enormous grizzly bears running toward him.

Medicine Bow Mountains: A mountain range in the Rockies

A full-grown grizzly weighs over 1,000 pounds and stands seven feet tall. Kit's gun was empty. What could he do now? He dropped his gun and ran for the nearest tall tree. The bears were in fast pursuit as Kit grabbed a tree branch and swung high into the tree. One of the bears, pawed at him, tearing off one of his moccasins. Kit knew bears could climb trees. He got out his hunting knife and held it ready. He cut off a branch to use as a club and hoped the tree was too small for the bears to climb. He struck at the male bear, who furiously charged and shook the tree in rage. Kit held on for dear life. The bear began tearing up

smaller trees and **bellowing**. It reached its paw for Kit. Kit used the club to smash a blow on the bear's nose. The animal yelped in pain, then left to join its mate, who was busily eating the elk. It was after midnight before Kit dared to drop to the ground and run for camp. The men were relieved to see him, sure that something had happened to him. Something had happened, and for the rest of his life, Kit would refer to his escape from the grizzlies as "my worst difficult experience."[61]

bellowing: Deeply roaring

A Celebration

In the summer of 1835, the trappers, traders, and friendly Native American people held a great get-together in the Green River Valley. They celebrated with horse races, shooting, and dancing. Kit Carson and his buddy Jim Bridger joined in the fun. Kit recognized a French-Canadian man who had a reputation for being a troublemaker. Kit found out that the troublemaker intended to steal the chief's daughter and take her with him. Kit confronted him and saved the girl, killing the bully in the process. The chief called for Kit the following day to thank him. Waa-nibe was the name of the chief's daughter. In time, she and Kit were married with the chief himself performing the marriage ceremony. Kit and Waa-nibe had a baby girl a year later and named her Adaline. The couple was happy.

Kit left on trapping expeditions in Blackfoot country and was successful wherever he went. One day, though, he got news that Waa-nibe was ill. He rushed home — 180 miles — on his beloved horse, only to have her die in his arms. Kit was heartbroken. He thought it best to take his little daughter to St. Louis to be raised by his sister. He hated the thought of leaving her, but his sister loved her like one of her own. He knew it was best for Adaline.

Meeting Fremont

Kit met Charles Fremont, who had been hired by the government to map out the Oregon Territory. Fremont had heard of Carson's reputation and took him on to help guide him. He offered to pay him $100 a month. So began a great friendship between the men. Carson saved Fremont's life several times. Charles Fremont was named "The Great Pathfinder," but Kit Carson was the "The Pathfinder's Pathfinder."

In his later years, Kit worked tirelessly for the welfare of the Native American people. In 1853, he served in the Office of Indian Affairs in Taos. He held this job for seven years. He worked to help other people understand the Native American communities. He devoted himself to the success of the Native American Treaty Commission. General John Pope said he was the best person in the country to work with Native Americans. "He is personally known and liked by every Indian of the bands likely to make trouble."[62] Kit Carson was an American frontiersman, trapper, soldier, and agent who made an outstanding contribution to the westward expansion of the United States. The capital city of Nevada is named after him.

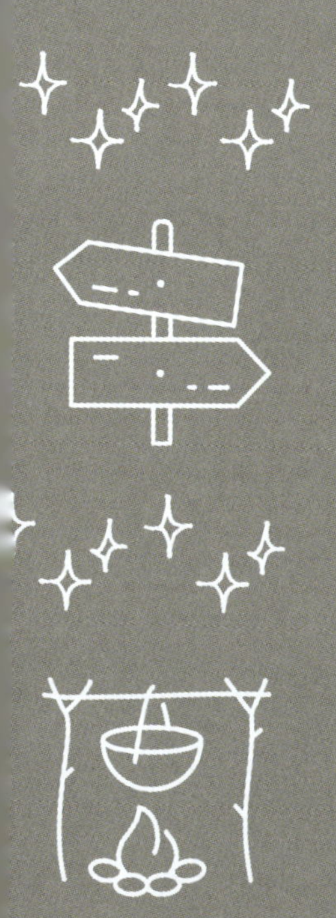

Jim Bridger – King of the Mountain Men

1804–1881	Virginia–Missouri

Who Was Jim Bridger?

Jim Bridger was born on March 17, 1804, in Richmond, Virginia. His father owned a good-sized farm and also ran a hotel. The family moved to St. Louis, Missouri, in 1812. Jim developed many skills that would define him in years to come. He spent many hours on the Mississippi River, exploring the area and handling his canoe. He developed a keen memory for learning and memorizing **terrain** such as bends in the river and landmarks that others might miss. He became very skilled at hunting with his gun.

terrain: Physical features of land

Four years after they moved, his mother died, and his aunt came to live with the family. In the fall of 1817, Jim's father died. So, at the age of 13, Jim was left an orphan. He felt responsible for providing for his younger sister. He got a job pumping the bellows for a blacksmith, and while there learned how to work with metal. Jim liked listening to the people who came into the blacksmith shop. Sometimes trappers who had been exploring out west came in. They told of beaver ponds with thousands of beavers. The trappers said they got good money for beaver pelts. People in Europe and America used beaver pelts to make oversized, tall hats.

Jim decided if another expedition started out, he would join it. He could send his money home to pay for his little sister's education.

Off to the West

When Jim was 18, he saw an ad from the Rocky Mountain Fur Company. They were looking for 100 men. Their job would be to follow the Missouri River to its source and trap beaver along the way. The company was owned by **General William Ashley**. They were to explore the Rocky Mountains under the command of Ashley's friend Andrew Henry. Henry had been one of the founders of the Missouri Fur Company and later joined forces with William Ashley to lead the expedition. Jim eagerly volunteered. At first, General Ashley thought he was too young, but finally decided to let him try. They left from St. Louis, Missouri, in April of 1822. Jim's sister and aunt came to see them off and wish them well.

They met with a lot of difficulty. Just after they started, one of their boats carrying $10,000 worth of essential supplies got its mast caught in a tree and **capsized**. Ashley

General William Ashley: Man credited with revolutionizing the fur trade by making it more efficient

capsized: Overturned

had to find another boat and reload it. Next, some of their horses were stolen, which forced them to stop and spend the winter at the mouth of the Yellowstone River, 1,800 miles from St. Louis.

They built a fort to protect themselves from the weather, wild animals, and unfriendly Native Americans. There they spent the winter hunting and trapping. The new men were paired up with the more experienced trappers. Jim's partner showed him how to set beaver traps. Each man carried with him six five-pound traps, his rifle, powder, shot, and a knife to skin beaver.

When they reached the beaver dam, the old trapper told Jim to wade out and set his trap near the **beaver lodge** as he had shown him. The water was bitterly cold. Jim was shivering before he got the trap set. In the morning, Jim found a beaver in his trap. As he reached down to **retrieve** it, he slipped and fell into the icy stream headfirst. He was cold to the bone, but excitedly brought his beaver to the old trapper to learn how to skin it.

beaver lodge: A beaver home built out of sticks, mud, and rocks

retrieve: Pick it up

More Trouble

That summer, a group of the men had to fight some Native Americans in Yellowstone country. They abandoned the fort they had built after 22 of their horses were stolen. The entire party of men changed their direction, moving to the Big Horn River to follow it to its source. The trappers camped for a while with the friendly Crow People. The chief was impressed with Jim and adopted him into the Crow tribe. He was given the name of Casapy, which meant "Chief of the Blankets."

Early the following spring, Jedediah Smith took a group of trappers from the Crow Village, trying to find a way to the Green River on the other side of the Rocky Mountains. One of the trappers he took with him was Jim Bridger, who was now about 20 years old. On this expedition they discovered the South Pass, which later provided passage for the covered wagons to roll through on the Oregon Trail.

The Great Salt Lake

Six months later, Jim had just finished supper with a group of trappers in Utah. They were talking around the campfire as the Bear River flowed slowly along. One of the trappers said he would sure like to see where that river goes. Some of the men speculated that it went north to the Snake River. Others thought it flowed into the Green River. Jim decided he wanted to find out who was right. The next morning, he began building a **bullboat**. He fashioned it from willow tree limbs, stretched buffalo hides over the limbs, and fastened them down. He finished by sewing the hides together tightly and pouring melted buffalo fat over the seams to make them watertight. He packed up some powder, shot, and dried buffalo meat for eating, climbed into his boat, and off he went. The trappers waved goodbye, but no one volunteered to join him.

bullboat: A tub-like vessel with buffalo hide

At first, the going was easy, but suddenly the rushing river pushed him into a **canyon**. The boat was tossed about and smashed into giant rocks. When the boat went flying out of the canyon, Jim managed to use his poles to get ashore.

canyon: A deep gorge with a river flowing through it

Climbing the steep rock wall, he could see a long way off. There was an open valley and mountains in the distance. He looked for signs of danger but saw none. Jim climbed higher up the steep wall and saw something silver glistening in the distance. He decided it must be a lake. He began to pole his boat down the Bear River, heading for the lake. Growing thirsty, he bent over the side of the boat to scoop up a drink of water. To his surprise, it was salty! Jim hollered, "This must be the Pacific Ocean!"

When Jim returned to the trappers in a few days, one of the men said, "Well, Jim, have you been to the Pacific Ocean and back already?"[63] Jim told them he actually had, and held out a bag of salt to prove it to the astonished trappers. What Jim had discovered, they found later, was not the Pacific Ocean but the Great Salt Lake. In later years, Salt Lake City would be built near this lake.

Yellowstone

After the long winter of trapping, Jim and a small group of trappers set out to explore again. This time they found the area later known as Yellowstone National Park. Jim's horse reared up when he approached a steaming **geyser**. Jim watched in amazement as the geyser hissed again, and water shot straight up. The water reached higher than a flagpole. Jim thought that no one would believe what he had seen. No one did believe it for some time. Late in 1830, Jim and his trappers left Yellowstone to explore the land to the south.

geyser: Rare hot spring that sends steam and water high into the air

They returned to Bear River and followed it to Salt Lake Valley, where they spent the winter trapping and hunting.

Stolen Horses

One night in March, a band of Bannock warriors raced into camp and left with 80 of the trappers' horses. Jim and some of his friends determined to get those horses back again, even if they had to walk to do it. They packed up dried meat, buffalo robes, and ammunition. Forty trappers set out trudging through the snow to retrieve the horses. It took them five days to spot the Bannock camp. Warriors were guarding 200–300 horses.

Jim and his buddy Tom Fitzpatrick split the men into two groups and prepared to charge the camp, hoping to scare off the horses. The men crawled along on their stomachs, quietly approaching the camp. When they got as close as possible, Jim shot his gun and all the trappers yelled loudly, waving their rifles in the air. The horses fled. Jim and the trappers each found a horse to jump on. They raced to safety before stopping to rest. All of the trappers were there; none had been wounded. Best of all, they had 120 horses to bring back to camp.

Jim Is Wounded

One day, Jim and his trappers met a group of Blackfeet warriors. The chief of the tribe rode up to Jim's horse and grabbed Jim's rifle by the barrel. He tried to pull it out of Jim's hand and the rifle went off into the air. As his horse turned, Jim heard the sound of a bowstring. Suddenly, his back felt as if it were on fire. An arrow sunk deep into his skin. Another one followed. Jim was knocked out of his saddle.

A battle **ensued** but Jim lay where he had fallen, two arrows in his back. After the battle, his buddy Tom tried to pull the arrows from his back. He gave Jim a piece of rawhide to bite to help him stand the pain as he pulled and pulled again. He was able to remove one arrow, but the other arrowhead stuck fast. For three years Jim carried that three-inch arrowhead in his back until he met Dr. Marcus Whitman, who finally removed it. It took a long time, and Jim had no pain medicine to help, but at last it came loose.

ensued: Took place

Jim Marries

Soon after this, Jim met and married Cora, daughter of a Flathead chief, who were a tribe of the Pacific Northwest. He took her to see Yellowstone for their honeymoon. All of Jim's trappers and Cora's father went with them, as well as some Flathead warriors. Jim and Cora were happy and soon had a baby daughter. They named her Mary Ann. About this time, something happened to the trapping trade. In Europe, tall silk hats were replacing beaver fur hats. The price for beaver pelts **plummeted.** Many of the mountain men began leaving the mountains. Wagon trains started to travel the Oregon Trail to settle California.

plummeted: Went down drastically

Fort Bridger

Jim knew that the settlers would need supplies, as well as someone to repair their wagons. In 1843, Jim decided to move to Wyoming and open a trading post. It was known as Fort Bridger. He built a high picket fence for protection. It became a popular spot for pioneers on their way to the West. Here they could trade for horses and oxen and hire guides to help them on their journey.

Sadly, three years after Jim started the fort, his wife Cora and their daughter Mary Ann died. After some time passed, Jim married again. His wife was of the Ute tribe. She died while giving birth to another daughter, named Virginia. Jim was married a third time to a Shoshone princess named Mary Washakie or "Little Fawn." Jim decided to move his family to Missouri and buy a farm to settle down.

Final Years

Jim spent many of his final years guiding wagon trains and serving as a guide to the United States Army. In 1868, Jim left the army and went back to his family and farm in Missouri. Jim was growing old and starting to go blind. He still had many happy times, though. He was famous for being a good storyteller. Neighborhood children loved to stop by his house to listen to his adventure stories.

Jim died when he was 77 years old. One of the old trappers who knew Jim wrote this about him: "He was the one man of the time that I never heard anything but good spoken of. I knew scores of hunters, scouts, and trappers .... The simplicity, gentleness, kindliness and absolute truthfulness of his character marked him as a man above the common.... There wasn't an Indian on the Overland Trail that doubted Jim Bridger's word."[64] Some have called Jim Bridger the "uncrowned king of all the Rocky Mountain scouts, trailers, and trappers."[65]

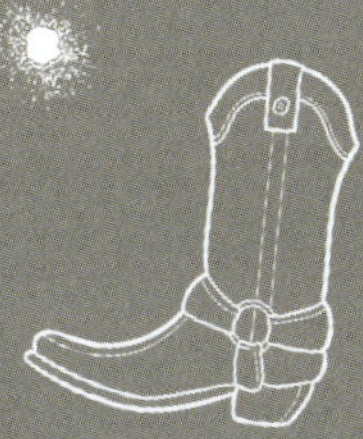

10

Wild Bill Hickok – Famous Lawman

1837–1876	Illinois–Dakota Territory

When the West was being settled, there was a great deal of violence and crime. Before law was established in the **territories**, many men saw an opportunity to profit at another's expense. A lawman's life, therefore, was in constant danger.

Who Was Bill Hickok?

James Butler Hickok grew up on a farm near the town of Troy Grove, Illinois. His father owned a small hotel named the Green Mountain House. James was ten years old when he had his first experience aiding his father to help some slaves escape to freedom. The Hickoks' house was one stop on the **Underground Railroad**. The Hickoks had a **trapdoor** in their kitchen floor. Here, they would hide escaped slaves and help them flee to the next stop. The goal was to help them get to the North and eventually Canada, where they would be free. James' mother would bake bread and pack venison, pickles, and apples for their journey.

territories: Land owned by a country but not yet organized into a state

Underground Railroad: Secret routes over which people helped slaves escape

trapdoor: A removable panel

James' father Alonzo Hickok had risked his life many times aiding men, women, and children on their flights to freedom. On this occasion, he was waiting for a suitable night to move some slaves to the next stop, Panton Mills, about 30 miles from the Hickok farm. This night was James' first time helping his father load the folks into the family wagon, cover them with quilts and sacks, and ride next to his father while he drove the horses.

It was a night James later said he never forgot. They had a close call. Men called them to stop so they could search the wagon, but Alonzo drove the horses faster. Shots were fired at the Hickoks, but they kept on. It was exciting for Jim. About dawn, they arrived at Panton Mills. James was sent to knock on the door of a modest-looking farmhouse. Alonzo helped three men and one woman into the house. The woman exclaimed, "Praise God Almighty! Praise God and His Underground Railroad!"[66]

After eating a bite of breakfast, the Hickoks prepared to go home. James remembered feeling like he'd been a part of something wonderful. This was not the first time or the last that the Hickoks helped others to freedom, but it was the first time James had "heard the whistle and zing of bullets close by. In the next 29 years he was to hear more than his share of such music."[67]

Wolf Hunter

Alonzo was in poor health and had trouble making ends meet as a farmer. James would help by hunting wolves. Wolves roamed the woods and plains and were a constant source of trouble for folks on the frontier settlements. They preyed on farm animals and killed hundreds of sheep, hogs, cattle, and even horses each year. The state offered a **bounty** for dead wolves. During the winter of 1849, he earned about $50 in bounty money. Jim also trapped and hunted along the Vermillion River near their home, supplying meat for the family's table. Jim purchased a new rifle with money he earned from 20 **muskrat pelts** and the skins of half a dozen **minks**. By the time Jim was 14, he was a better shot than most grown men.

bounty: A monetary payment

muskrat pelts: Soft brownish-gray fur of rodents

minks: Small furry animals

The Hickoks were a happy family. During the evening, the children studied while Mrs. Hickok cleaned up the kitchen after supper. Alonzo would tell stories to the children when they finished their lessons. Jim loved his father's stories. The children would talk about what they wanted to do when they grew up. Jim always said he would live in the West. His father told him life was hard in the West because there was no law and order. Jim said maybe when he was older he could help bring law

and order to the West. His father said, "James, if you must go West, all I ask is that you always be on the side of law and order. Be a man."[68] Jim promised his father that he would.

Off for the West

In 1852, Alonzo Hickok grew ill and died, leaving six children to be cared for. Fifteen-year-old James got a job driving **freighting teams** for a local shop owner. When he was 17, a canal needed to be dug in the area, and Jim was hired as a laborer for better wages. When Jim was 18, he asked his mother for permission to finally go west. She reminded him of his promise to his father. "Wherever you go, my son, whatever you do, my prayers will follow you."[69]

freighting teams: Men who drove wagons and guarded the freight

Jim walked almost 300 miles to St. Louis, Missouri, armed with his pistol, rifle, and hunting knife. He had a small pack of clothes, food on his back, and a few dollars. In St. Louis, there was much talk about Kansas. It had become a battleground for the pro-slavery and anti-slavery groups. There would be trouble for sure. Remembering his family's work in helping **fugitives** escape, Jim was determined to go to Kansas.

fugitives: Escaped people who are in hiding

Jim was offered a job on a farm working for a man named John Owens, a few miles west of Leavenworth, Kansas. Jim worked hard and sent money back home to his mother. Jim liked the Owens family, and they came to love him too. The farmer's wife was a Shawnee woman.

Jim was fascinated with Native American customs and learned much from Mrs. Owens. He learned cures for sicknesses, how to prepare foods of the Native People, and how to make clothes. He decided to let his hair grow long as the Native Americans do and never cut it again. The things he learned from the Owens would be useful to him his whole life. John Owens and Jim Hickok took part in the dangerous job of shipping hundreds of rifles to Leavenworth to distribute to Northern **sympathizers**. As a result, Kansas was brought into the Union on the side of the North.

sympathizers: Supporters

One day, Jim heard of a shooting match to be held. He decided to enter to try to win the prize of $100. He won hands down, and soon, everyone was praising him for his marksmanship.

Stage Coach Driver

In 1858, when Jim was 21, he was chosen to be a **constable** by the settlers of Monticello, Kansas. As a result, it wasn't long before Monticello was known for being unusually law-abiding. The Reed Hotel in Monticello was a stop on the **stage** route between Topeka, Kansas, and eastern Kansas. Whenever a driver was sick, Jim would be asked to drive the stage. He found he really liked the job. In the summer of 1859, he moved west again and began driving a stage from Independence, Missouri, to Santa Fe, New Mexico. The trail led over the Rocky Mountains, which was a very rough path. He built a reputation for his skillful driving. He met other mountain men such as Kit Carson, and made many friendships.

constable: A peace officer

stage: A horse-drawn coach that carries passengers

One night on the trail, Jim was attacked by a grizzly bear. He managed to kill it with his knife, but not before he was badly hurt. A few hours later, a wagon train came along the trail and found Jim unconscious with the bear partly on top of him. Jim was barely alive. Fortunately, the wagon driver recognized him and brought him to Santa Fe for treatment.

Wild Bill

Jim needed some time to recover from his wounds. By the time he had regained his strength and the use of his badly damaged arm, the Civil War had begun. Jim had made good friends on both sides, but he knew which side he must help. He headed for **Fort Leavenworth** where he joined the army and was put in charge of a special wagon train. The wagon train was loaded with supplies bound for Union soldiers stationed at Sedalia, Missouri. The train was captured by Confederate soldiers on the way, but Jim managed to escape and tried to get help. Riding to Independence, Missouri, he was told no troops were available there; he should try Kansas City. Jim was tired and so was his horse. He knew he'd have to find somewhere to sleep before making that trip.

Fort Leavenworth: The oldest settlement in Kansas

The town of Independence was full of unrest that night. There were gangs of rough men causing trouble. The constable was in hiding, fearing for his life. Jim knew something must be done. He jumped on a fence and shouted at the angry mob, telling them to go home. An old veteran of the Santa Fe trail recognized Jim and began praising him to the mob. A crowd began to gather, the troublemakers cooled down, and soon people were praising Jim for stopping the angry mob. In the crowd were some women; one of them, for some reason, hollered, "Good for you, Wild Bill!"[70] No one knows why, but the name stuck. Word spread, and from then on, quiet, modest Jim Butler Hickok was known as "Wild Bill Hickok." Jim always said he never liked that name and would rather be called Jim, but it was not to be.

Jim slept in a stable with his horse that night. In the morning, he made the trip to Kansas City, secured the help of 100 **cavalrymen**, and managed to overtake the wagon train, recapturing the supplies. "Wild Bill" had accomplished his first task of the war.

cavalrymen: Soldiers on horseback

Union Scout

Wild Bill's reputation went before him. He was asked to scout for the Union, which was the most dangerous job in the army. He pretended to be a farmhand trying to join up with the Confederate Army but was recognized by a Confederate corporal as "Wild Bill." He was sentenced to be hung the following morning. Realizing the danger he was in, he overpowered the man who was guarding him during the night.

Jim put on the guard's clothes, took his rifle, and escaped into the woods. "Wild Bill" walked all night and managed to arrive safely back in Union lines by morning. He gave the information he had been sent to learn: there was a massive supply of gunpowder being stored at Yellville, Arkansas. "Wild Bill" was chosen to lead a raid. The gunpowder was burned, rifles captured, and more than 100 horses taken. "Wild Bill" was acclaimed for his exceptional work. Over the next two years, he had many tough assignments as a scout.

Deputy Marshal

When the war ended, there was a new motivation for men to move west again. The Homestead Act was passed, which assured a man 160 acres of land for free if he would agree to settle on it and make certain improvements. Many honest, hardworking people moved west. Unfortunately, so did lawbreakers who wanted to **prey** on honest folks. It would be some time before states, counties, and towns were established in the West.

prey: Plunder

Jim was given the job of United States deputy marshal and assigned to **Fort Riley**, Kansas. Jim found that law and order was almost nonexistent. In one month, 84 army horses had been stolen. After only two days at Fort Riley, Jim set out alone. Six days later he returned to the fort with nine army mules and two **deserters**.

Fort Riley: An army camp in north central Kansas

deserters: Soldiers who run away and don't intend to return

He set out again with four soldiers and soon returned with more than 200 army horses and mules. The general at the fort thought it odd and asked if the horses were just loose or in someone's possession. Jim affirmed that there were some bad-looking fellows "up the valley apiece."[71] The general never could get the whole story of how Jim accomplished this feat. "They sort of tried to stop us but they didn't. And they're not likely to trouble you anymore."[72] The general laughed, realizing Hickok was one of the shyest, most modest men in the West. However, he did it, he had managed to clean out a nest of horse thieves. Discipline at Fort Riley began to improve greatly.

Hays City

Jim's next job was as marshal of Hays City, Kansas. The settlement had been growing rapidly, and honest citizens were being threatened by violence from criminals. Jim accepted the assignment. He patrolled the streets with his weapons slung over his arm. One night as Marshal Hickok was making his rounds, a lawbreaker stepped out from a doorway and aimed his **cocked** gun at him. He said, "Hickok, I've got you now. I'll give you one minute to say your prayers."[73] Jim, looking over the man's shoulder, called out, "Don't hit him, Andy!"[74] The man immediately turned to see "Andy," who didn't really exist. In that instant, Jim shot him dead. When news of the fearless lawman got around, criminals realized they would have to change their ways or leave Hays City. Newspapers in Boston, Massachusetts, and New York reported that violence was a thing of the past in Hays City.

cocked: Ready to shoot

The Rush for Gold

Jim continued to rid the West of lawbreakers. In the spring of 1876, Jim, now 39 years old, was offered $1,000 to be the guide for a group of men headed to the Black Hills in South Dakota. Their purpose was to search for recently discovered gold. Jim agreed to guide the men as long as he was in command

and could maintain the discipline of the group. While there, he was offered the job of marshal at Deadwood Gulch in the Black Hills. He turned it down. He recognized more than 200 criminals in the place. He commented that the Black Hills was the most dangerous section of the United States at that time.

Two outlaws in Deadwood Gulch, a narrow valley area, plotted to kill Jim. They feared he might change his mind and accept the marshal job. If he did that, he would be sure to clean the town of outlaws as he had at Hays City. They bribed another man to do the job, telling him he would be the most famous man in the West if he killed Wild Bill.

Jim always had the habit of sitting with his back toward a wall and facing the door so he could keep an eye on people entering and therefore be alert to danger. For some reason, he had his back to the door that night. Slipping up behind him as he was sitting at the table, the man shot him from a distance of only three feet. Jim Hickok, the famous "Wild Bill," slumped over on the table, dead. The shooter, John McCall was arrested, tried, and hanged for the murder.

“Few men did more to bring law and order to the West than Wild Bill Hickok. When the odds were against him, he wore the silver star with honor. His adventurous life is a story of never-failing courage and of honesty never questioned.”[75] Jim had indeed honored the promise he made years ago to his father.

Glossary

adamant: Unshakable in his position

agility: Skillfulness

ambushed: Attacked from a concealed position

assemblyman: Member of a committee that makes laws

asset: Valuable

avert: Avoid

barrel staves: Narrow lengths of wood used to form barrels

bayonets: Blades attached to the muzzle of a rifle

beaver lodge: A beaver home built out of sticks, mud, and rocks

bellowing: Deeply roaring

bellows: Device for blowing on a fire

blacksmith: Person who makes and repairs things made of iron

blockhouse: Observation tower

bountiful: Plentiful

bounty: A monetary payment

buckskin: Made from the skin of a deer

bullboat: A tub-like vessel covered with buffalo hide

cache: A pit dug in the ground

canyon: A deep gorge with a river flowing through it

capsized: Overturned

caravan: A group of people traveling together

cascades: Small waterfalls

casting: Making in a mold

cavalrymen: Soldiers on horseback

circumvent: Go around

coaxed: Persuaded

cocked: Ready to shoot

colonel: An officer of high rank

condensed: A thick stock to which you add water

constable: A peace officer

coonskin cap: A hat made from the skin and fur of a raccoon

Corps of Discovery: An expedition exploring the Louisiana Purchase

depot: Storehouse

deserters: Soldiers who run away and don't intend to return

devastated: Heartbroken and discouraged

dilemma: Problem

dwindle: Get low

ensued: Took place

expedition: A journey or voyage

flash flood: A sudden flood due to heavy rainfall

flax: Flowering plant for linen production

Fort Leavenworth: The oldest settlement in Kansas

Fort Riley: An army camp in north central Kansas

fraught: Filled

freight: A vessel carrying goods

freighting teams: Men who drove wagons and guarded the freight

fugitives: Escaped people who are in hiding

garrison: A military post

General William Ashley: Man credited with revolutionizing the fur trade by making it more efficient

geyser: Rare hot spring that sends steam and water high into the air

hairy bank notes: Pelts worth money

headquarters: Center of operations

hickory stick: A stick used to deliver a spanking

indebted: Something borrowed that has to be repaid

jaundice: When someone's liver is not working properly

Jim Bowie: A pioneer and soldier

justice of the peace: A person appointed to act as judge

Kaskaskians: Native Americans who were from the area we call Illinois

keelboat: A long, narrow boat with pointed ends

kegs: Barrels

lard: Fat used in cooking

looking glasses: Mirrors

lull: Temporary quiet time

marveled: Were filled with astonishment

Medicine Bow Mountains: A mountain range in the Rockies

militia: Civilian military force

minks: Small furry animals

moccasins: Soft leather shoes made by Native Americans

mockirsons: Clark's spelling of moccasins

Mojave: Native American tribe

muskrat pelts: Soft brownish-gray fur of rodents

negotiations: Discussions meant to reach an agreement

oath of allegiance: Promise of loyalty

obligated: Committed

oppressive: Unjustly hard

pace: Speed

parched: Dry

paved: Opened up

pear cactus: A prickly plant

pelts: Animal skins

plummeted: Went down drastically

prey: Plunder

procuring: Obtaining

Providence: God's guidance

recruit: Find men to join

Red Sticks: Named for their red-painted war clubs

ransomed: Released after paying money

rapids: Dangerously fast-flowing waters

reconnoitering: Group of men sent to gather information

reinforcements: Extra soldiers

reputation: Good name

resided: Lived

resolve: Determination

retire: Leave his job

retrieve: Pick it up

ruthless: Showing no compassion

salt springs: Saltwater springs

sandbars: Areas of shallow sand in the water

sandstone bluff: A steep shoreline slope formed of rock made of quartz sand

scouts: Men sent ahead to gather information

spellbound: Fascinated

stage: A horse-drawn coach that carries passengers

staunch: Committed

stockade: A fortification around a town

stockade fence: Protective barrier

submerged: Covered with water

sure shots: Skilled in shooting

surmised: Guessed

surveying: Establishing boundaries for a plot of land

sympathizers: Supporters

terrain: Physical features of land

territories: Land owned by a country but not yet organized into a state

tomahawk: A single-handed ax

translated: Interpreted

trapdoor: A removable panel

truce: A cease-fire

uncharted: Unfamiliar

Underground Railroad: Secret routes over which people helped slaves escape

valiant: Brave

Wabash River: The southward flowing tributary of the Ohio River

The Wilderness Road: The path through Cumberland Gap that Daniel Boone had created

William Travis: The lieutenant colonel of the cavalry for the Texan army

Corresponding Curriculum

The *What a Character! Series* can be used alongside other Master Books curriculum for reading practice or to dive deeper into topics that are of special interest to students.

This book in the series features famous pioneers and frontiersmen, whose stories would incorporate well for students in grades 6–8 accompanying history, language arts, vocabulary words and definitions, as well as geography studies and cultural insights. We have provided the list below to help match this book with related Master Books curriculum.

Chapters 1–9

America's Story Vol. 1

Children's Atlas of the U.S.A.

Elementary U.S. Geography & Social Studies

Language Lessons for a Living Education

Chapter 10

America's Story Vol. 2

Children's Atlas of the U.S.A.

Elementary U.S. Geography & Social Studies

Language Lessons for a Living Education

Endnotes

1. Roy Nemerson, *Daniel Boone* (New York: Baronet Books, 1946), 67.
2. Ibid. 68.
3. Sydelle Kramer, *Who Was Daniel Boone?* (New York: Penguin Random House, 2006), 26.
4. Nemerson, *Daniel Boone,* 62.
5. Kramer, *Who Was Daniel Boone*? 48
6. Ibid., 58.
7. Ibid., 69.
8. John Mason Brown, *Daniel Boone, The Opening of the Wilderness* (New York: Random House, 1952), 176.
9. Adele de Leeuw, *George Rogers Clark* (Champaign, Illinois: Garrard Publishing Co., 1967), 12.
10. Lawton B. Evans, *America First: One Hundred Stories from Our Own History* (Springfield, Massachusetts: Milton Bradley Company, 1926), 218.
11. Russell Roberts, *The Life and Times of George Rogers Clark* (Hockessin, Delaware: Mitchell Lane Publishers, 2007), 20.
12. Evans, 217.
13. Ibid., 220.
14. Ibid., 220.
15. de Leeuw, *George Rogers Clark*, 69.
16. Ibid., 76.
17. Ibid., 71.
18. Ibid., 80.
19. Zane Grey, *Betty Zane* (Digreads.com Publishing, 2019), 10.
20. Ibid., 24.
21. Lawton B. Evans, *America First: One Hundred Stories from Our Own History* (Springfield, Massachusetts: Milton Bradley Company, 1920), 166.
22. Ibid., 168.
23. Grey, *Betty Zane,* 189.
24. Ibid., 189.
25. Ibid., 191.
26. Gail Herman, *Who Was Davy Crockett?* (New York: Penguin Random House, 2013), 27.
27. Ibid., 32.
28. Ibid., 43.
29. Enid Lamonte Meadowcroft, *The Story of Davy Crockett* (Columbus, Ohio: Weekly Reader Books, 1952), 135.
30. Elizabeth Moseley, *Davy Crockett: Hero of the Wild Frontier* (Philadelphia, Pennsylvania: Chelsea House Publishers, 1991), 54.
31. Ibid., 68.
32. Meadowcroft, *The Story of Davy Crockett,* 161.
33. Ibid., 72.
34. Dale Morgan, *Jedediah Smith and the Opening of the West* (New York: Bobbs-Merrill Co., 1953), 25.
35. Frank Latham, *Jed Smith* (Champaign, Illinois: Garrard Publishing Company, 1968), 16.
36. Ibid., 20.
37. Ibid., 40.
38. Ibid., 41.
39. Ibid., 41.
40. Ibid., 51.
41. Ibid., 54.
42. Jedediah Smith, *Jedediah Smith's Journal: The First Expedition to California*, 7 August 1826–3 July 1827.
43. Ibid.

44. John Bakeless, *The Adventures of Lewis and Clark* (New York: Dover Publications, 2002), 29.
45. Judith St. George, *What Was the Lewis and Clark Expedition?* (New York: Penguin Random House, 2014), 9.
46. Ibid., 43.
47. Ibid., 62.
48. Ibid., 98.
49. Ibid., 104.
50. Mary Blount Christian, *Who'd Believe John Colter?* (New York: Macmillan Publishing Co., 1993), 19.
51. Ibid., 20.
52. Ibid., 39.
53. Ibid., 40.
54. Ibid., 41.
55. Evans, *America First*, 252.
56. Ibid., 252.
57. Nardi Reeder Campion, *Kit Carson: Pathfinder of the West* (Champaign, Illinois: Garrard Publishing Company, 1963), 28.
58. Ibid., 33–34.
59. Ibid., 49.
60. Ibid., 49.
61. Ibid., 58.
62. Ibid., 77.
63. Willard and Celia Luce, *Jim Bridger—Man of the Mountains* (New York: Chelsea House Publishers, 1991), 46.
64. Grace Raymond Hebard and E.A. Brininstool, *Jim Bridger: The Grand Old Man of the Rockies* (Mount Pleasant, South Carolina: Arcadia Press, 2017), 41.
65. Ibid., 54.
66. Stewart. H. Holbrook, *Wild Bill Hickok Tames the West* (New York: Random House, 1955), 11.
67. Ibid., 12.
68. A.M. Anderson, *Wild Bill Hickok* (New York: Harper and Row Publishers, 1960), 11.
69. Ibid., 15.
70. Holbrook, *Wild Bill Hickok Tames the West,* 58.
71. Ibid., 82.
72. Ibid., 83.
73. Ibid., 100.
74. Ibid., 100.
75. Anderson, *Wild Bill Hickok,* introduction.